# DEAD LUCKY

# DEAD LUCKY

## AN AUTOBIOGRAPHY

As told to Alan Watts

## LIONEL DUNNING

ARTHUR BARKER LIMITED
LONDON

A subsidiary of Weidenfeld (Publishers) Ltd

ISBN 0 213 16911 8

Typeset at The Spartan Press Ltd
Lymington, Hants
Printed in Great Britain by Butler & Tanner Ltd
Frome and London

# Contents

# Illustrations

Except where otherwise indicated, the photographs in this
book are from the author's own collection.

# 1 Death in the Ring

I am Lionel Dunning the show jumper who, until recently, lay fourth in the national rankings, but in my time have worked as a coalman, truck driver, car assembly worker and farrier. I have scaled the heights and touched the lowest ebbs that any human being might be asked to do. I have called the story of my life *Dead Lucky* because, despite all that has happened to me and all the slings and arrows that fortune has directed at me, I still feel I am lucky even to be alive today. I have learned the hard way to fight back against the awful problems that life some-times presents. And now, after a long time fending for myself, I have a loving wife who is also an international show jumper and with whom I vie for top honours in that rough, tough world. We have a son who is the apple of his Daddy's eye and a yard which houses some of the most promising horses in the country. How I made it into show jumping, why I feel I am lucky to be alive, and how, as I write this, I wonder if my luck has deserted me, I will now tell you.

Show jumping may look like a glamorous sport to the TV audience, but believe me it can also be a killer. It 'killed' me once, and that resulted from an error I made in August 1975 during a round at the Greater London Horse Show on Clapham Common. My top horse then was Union Jack, a six-year-old grey thoroughbred gelding, and the fatal jump was at the sixth fence in the course.

We had made a good job of the first five fences, but it had been raining prior to the competition and the going was slippery in places. Fence six was a big triple-bar, five feet high and with a six-foot spread – not all that large by today's standards, but certainly formidable. I still don't know quite why Union Jack's hindquarters skidded from under him during the take-off, but the fact is we just did not take off properly and the horse went straight into the fence. If the fence had been an upright one, there would have been no problem, but the sloping nature of the triple bar meant that as the horse stopped and my hard hat came off I was on my way to collision with a wing.

I hit the wing like a shell from a gun, and then oblivion. I landed, unconscious, in the middle of the fence and the poles came down on top of me. What unfortunately didn't help was that, as a result of my automatic reaction not to let go of my horse, my hand was still twisted up with the reins. Union Jack was struggling to get up and constantly tugging at my immobile arm, pulling it from its socket. They tell me that before they could free him he had added his struggling weight to the pile of poles that were pinning me down.

My wife Pam was there watching all this happen since she was due in the ring next. Now Pam is pretty phlegmatic – you have to be in this game – but when I did not appear to move she knew that this was no ordinary fall.

With the arena party and others trying to release the horse and clear the debris of the fence from me, Pam (and others) thought that she was now a widow. It was Dr Mandell Hodgson, the British Show Jumping Association's honorary medical officer, who brought me back to life – because technically I was dead. I apparently had no pulse and I was not breathing. You only need to be in that state for a few minutes and you are a certain goner.

However, it was absolutely dead lucky that Hodgson had his oxygen resuscitation equipment with him and, after he had massaged my heart and blown life-giving oxygen into my inert lungs, I began to breathe and flickered back to life. Then it was hospital at Balham and head X-rays and intensive care.

Of course I knew nothing about any of this, for I was still out cold and that is how I remained the next day and the day after. During that time there was no guarantee that I would ever regain consciousness. When you think of how poor Hartwig Steenken lay for weeks after the tragic accident that ended his life of show jumping, then it is possible to realize what doubts and fears coursed through Pam's mind as she watched my inert body and waited for some sign that I was going to come back from oblivion.

Not that Pam spent every moment at my bedside. You get to

the top of any sport by ruthless application to the job in hand.
Pam had to prove that it was not some fault of the horse that
had led to the fall, and so the day following the accident she
went back to Clapham Common and rode Union Jack in the
competition for which he was entered.

Pam did not usually ride Jack as he was a very powerful
handful of horse, but despite having what is called in certain
quarters an 'interesting round' she managed to go clear on him
even if he went at something more than the recommended pace
for these events. That Pam rode at all caused a furore amongst
those of our friends and acquaintances who thought my wife
was being very callous, but she knew that I would have done
the same thing myself if the circumstances had been reversed.
The biggest lesson of all that living a constantly dangerous life
teaches you is that there is no room for false emotions and
motives. You look your problems straight in the eye and act
accordingly.

Even when I regained consciousness, I was still at sixes and
sevens from the blow to my head. I just about knew that Pam
was there, but in my poor befuddled brain chaos reigned and
this state of affairs was not helped at all by the fact that I
couldn't focus properly. The concussion had affected my vision
so that I could not see straight and what I could see was
blurred.

They kept me in the hospital for a fortnight and then sent me
back home to Lincolnshire with the rather facile advice to take
it easy. There wasn't much else I could do as I was as weak as a
kitten and I still couldn't focus properly. Even more of a
problem in the long term was my arm, which had been
fractured and which I couldn't move. I could imagine that time
would pull my sight back to some form of normality, but with
an immobile arm I would be out of show jumping for ever. Days
passed, weeks passed, and no improvement came that was
worth talking about.

So it was back under the X-ray machine. Then they
discovered something that one might have imagined was the
problem from the first – the shoulder was dislocated. I suppose
you shouldn't always believe medics when they pontificate
about what you've got wrong with you, but we had assumed

that the initial diagnosis was correct. If the dislocation had been put right straightaway, the arm would have come back to some kind of mobility on its own. As it was, in the weeks that had passed since the accident the muscles had knitted up in such a way that my whole arm was held in an abnormal position. That entailed an operation, and it proved to be a big problem for the surgeons. They took four whole hours to get my shoulder back to where it ought to have been and even then they had to fix it with a steel pin.

They took out the pin after three weeks – three more weeks for my arm to continue withering so that I had no power over it at all. It just hung there like a string girth when you have just put the saddle on and haven't yet girthed up. It didn't help much when I recalled the parting words of the surgeon: 'I don't know how much you'll be able to move the shoulder, but I've done all I can. The rest is up to you.'

The next few weeks were torture. Not so much physical – although that was bad enough – but mental. Trying to face the prospect that my consuming passion was no more. Perhaps I would ride again, but when you have pitted yourself against the big courses and the big names, the idea of a bit of hacking holds little appeal. Anyway I still couldn't see straight and you cannot ride at fences without spot-on vision. Scaling fences which are close to the maximum that the horse can manage at the pace that is set in competitions of international standard is a question of co-ordination of hand and eye and split-second timing. There is no room for error when the fences get over five feet high.

There was also another problem that really bothered me. I couldn't remember things properly and even if I could get the useless arm to function again, I would be constantly eliminated for taking the wrong course because I couldn't remember which fence came next. Sussing out the course is difficult enough when you are fully alert, especially indoors where maybe a dozen individual fences follow one another along the incredibly tortuous path that the course-builder has set in order to give the course sufficient length. But I comforted myself with the thought that maybe my memory problem was due to the tranquillizers that I had to take.

However even if that was the case, there were worse things happening in the yard. I wasn't earning anything and the hospital fees cost a packet. Despite the fact that Pam was still riding and winning all this time, it was not bringing in half enough money to keep us going. It was heart-breaking for us to see so many of our horses being sold because we could not afford to keep them. We also had to give one of our grooms the sack, which we were very loath to do. It was a time of the most abject despair, but not yet as deep a despair as was to follow my fight back.

That deepest of deep depressions followed my fight back. I don't know what separated the day I knew I had to get up off my backside, stop feeling sorry for myself, and take up cudgels against my affliction, from the day before, but I do remember the day I decided I would ride again. In retrospect it doesn't seem much different from any other of those druggy days, but it was for me a turning point. If anyone else is in the same situation, I say to them: don't give in. Despite the impossibility of scaling Everest with only one arm, get stuck into it. I did, and now I will tell you how.

## 2 The Struggle Back to Life

Before I continue this story of woe, let me just go back a little. I remember being brought home from Balham Hospital and walking around for several days complaining that my left shoulder hurt. Eventually Pam persuaded me to go and have an X-ray in Newark Hospital. I remember driving there with great difficulty because I only really had the use of my right hand, but the car was my father-in-law's automatic which was a little easier for me to drive and I could just manage it on my own. I went to the hospital and there they told me that I had a very badly fractured and dislocated shoulder, and the doctor immediately arranged for me to be transferred to Harlow Wood Orthopaedic Hospital near Mansfield. Well I came out of the hospital feeling very very low and I drove the car home. There Pam packed me a suitcase and drove me to Harlow Wood thinking that all I was going in for was a minor operation to my arm.

In the end I had the operation, but it was not at all minor. In fact it was very serious. When Pam came to see me she was appalled at what they had had to do. I was a mass of bandages and out of them stuck the end of a four-inch pin which was holding the shoulder joint in place. The rest of my arm was suspended in mid-air so that it couldn't move and ruin the surgical work.

There followed three further weeks of total immobility before they were able to take the pin out and again my arm just hung there. I was totally unable to move it at all. The muscles had wasted and on leaving the hospital I was told that I would never be able to drive a car or ride a horse again. I came home, driven by my father-in-law, in a dazed condition. I was physically weak and incapable of doing anything.

At night I would have to get up continually to ease the pain in my shoulder, so my poor wife wasn't getting any sleep and I had to move out into the spare bedroom. Just to show you how weak I was, one night I had to get up to spend a penny, which meant going to the *en suite* bathroom – through our bedroom where Pam was sleeping, together with our curly coated retriever dogs. They are gentle pets, but they are also prepared to have a go when they think danger threatens. Never having had anyone come into the room from outside in the middle of the night, the moment I began to push the door open the dogs flung themselves against it and, unable to maintain my balance in my weakened condition, I fell over backwards. Luckily it didn't do any more harm to my arm but it certainly gave me – and the dogs – a fright, not to mention Pam who was suddenly awakened by the commotion.

Now not only did I have this useless arm, but to make matters worse I was told I had a blood clot in it which the doctors said would later have to be removed. Well, when I got home I started slowly trying to make my arm work, because I knew full well that if I were ever to get back into the show jumping ring the arm had to function again. In my case the 'no foot – no horse' saying became 'no arm – no jockey'. To this end I would use any kind of device to get my arm moving. I would sit at the table, in my arm chair, anywhere, and, using a rope attached to a spur-strap round my left wrist, I would pull my arm up and down. If you go into our lounge and kitchen today, there are, in various places, the remains of rings and nails on which Pam suspended pulleys for the ropes.

Slowly, oh so slowly, with my good arm I began to pull some degree of mobility back into my dead one and eventually I began to move it again. As well as the other exercises, I used to lie on the floor and attempt to lift light things. I started off with small ornaments and worked up to full bags of sugar.

This began to pay off and soon I had my arm working a bit. Pam used to drive me into Lincoln most days to visit a physiotherapist, but progress was agonizingly slow and often I despaired of ever getting back the use of my arm. Then one day I achieved a break-through. I reached up and switched on a light. Such a small thing to most people, but to me it was fantastic. I remember rushing out into the yard shouting, 'Pam! Pam! I'm winning.' It was a great boost to my morale –

and Pam's – because it showed that there was a good chance I could get much more mobility into the arm.

With this increased confidence I became more venturesome. I was fed up with being chauffeured around by my wife and so one day, unbeknown to her, I slipped into her car, tied my bad left arm to the wheel so that it was forced to move with it as I drove, and fighting against the pain I drove into Lincoln which is just twelve short miles up the road from home. That journey occupied no less than six times the usual fifteen minutes it normally took, and I was in a bit of a state when I got there, I can tell you, but I had done it. To hell with my erratic vision. If my eyesight went a bit peculiar for a while I just drove more slowly. Luckily the minor road to Lincoln was fairly deserted and I could go at my own, often snail's, pace. From then on I drove to Lincoln whenever I wished.

As well as going to the physiotherapist, I was going to a Mr Harwell from Wisbech. He was a very clever man, a nerve specialist, and I had gone to see if he could help me. One day he was exercising my shoulder and a little more life was returning to it. I pointed out this clot in the vein that I had and I told him that the doctors had told me I was going to have to have it removed.

'Don't be so ridiculous,' he said. 'That's not a clot in the vein at all. You've got a nerve trapped in your wrist.' With that this remarkable man massaged my wrist.

'This is going to hurt,' he said as he manipulated it with sympathetic but expert hands. He was dead right – it certainly did.

'Not to worry my boy,' he said. 'Now the pain and trouble will slowly disappear.' I had been going to Mr Harwell for perhaps two to three months, and like a fool I'd never mentioned this problem until now. All that time I had been treating the arm myself every night with a preparation which is rubbed on patients' legs when they have varicose veins to relieve pain and tension. But that stuff had done me no good at all.

I came home from that fateful session and had the best night's sleep I'd had in months and, to my absolute astonishment, when I woke up next morning the so-called clot in the vein had completely disappeared. Mr Harwell had with his experience noted immediately what the trouble was – something that the doctors had completely missed – a nerve trapped in my left wrist from when I had my accident. Once he had repositioned the nerve, it relieved the blood supply and the trouble cleared up and has never returned.

Without Pam knowing, because she'd never have let me go if she had – though I hadn't told even her just how bad my eyesight was – I started to ride. At that time Pam was riding a horse that belonged to Barry and Vida Baldock called Windsong, and I had another horse called Call Me Sam. He was the horse on which I had my second bad accident in July 1977 at the Royal Agricultural Show when I badly damaged the cartilage in my right leg.

I wasn't up to top show jumping – maybe any form of show jumping – but I had to get back, and of course I went too fast and too far too soon. What happened was that coming up to a combination my eyesight went again and I lost sight of the fence completely. The horse knew that I wanted to stop so he stopped, but I sailed on to hit the ground beyond the fence. I knew pretty well what had happened when I heard my knee crack as I hit the ground.

I was taken from the ring at the Royal Show in an ambulance to Warwick Hospital where they X-rayed the knee and told me I had just ricked it badly. Then they sent me back to the show and under great pain we went out for a meal with Tony and Maureen Holden and Marion and David Mould, which Pam had arranged as she had no idea that my injury was as bad as it subsequently proved to be.

What a fool to be so impatient. I was now ten times worse off than before. I had made good progress and if I'd left it a while longer maybe all would have been well. As it was, I was now on crutches, my shoulder still ached, my memory was still faulty and the new fall seemed to have shaken up whatever it was that was clouding my vision. Anyway the eyesight problem was now worse. I don't know if I have ever felt more down and hopeless than at that time. I truly thought I was finished.

I kept hobbling around for the next six weeks, with the aid of a walking stick. I still had a whole load of young riders coming to me to be trained and I was having to train them from the ground. Then one day I had a phone call from a man called Mr Plaster asking if his son Ian could come and have a few days' tuition with me. I'd helped him in the past, but he asked if I could do some revision with Ian and help him a bit more. He had a good grey horse which used to be ridden by Brian Crocker.

After his few days' tuition were up, his father came to pick him up. Seeing the predicament I was in, he told me that his next-door neighbour, Mr Alan Letting, was the chief surgeon at an orthopaedic hospital in London

Mr Plaster arranged for me to go and see Mr Letting. It was close to the late summer bank holiday at the end of August when I went to see him. Before I went, I decided to arm myself with the evidence and I got my vet – yes, my vet – to X-ray my knee. I saw Mr Letting one Thursday afternoon. He examined my knee, took one look at the X-rays and asked me to drop everything and go into hospital that very day to have the knee operated on.

I said that that was impossible as I had several pupils in the middle of their training schedules, including Vicky Baldock with Bombadillo which had not yet qualified for Wembley. The pony had to win one of the Christy Beaufort classes and there was only one qualifier left to take part in. That was the one at the Town and Country Festival which was held at the Royal Show Ground at Stoneleigh. However it was all rather difficult as Mr Letting was due to go on holiday on the Wednesday after the bank holiday. He was very good about it and volunteered to put his holiday back one day so that I could finish the training I was engaged in.

I went with Vicky to the Town and Country Festival on the Sunday, and Bombadillo not only qualified but actually won the Regional Final there. So having done all I could and helped Vicky to success I came home and on the Tuesday I packed the few things I needed and took the train to London. St Luke's Hospital for the Clergy is in Fitzroy Square just near the Post Office Tower and there I was admitted and forced to starve for twelve hours. That is how they make sure you are fit for an operation, and on the Wednesday – when he should have been on holiday – Mr Letting operated on my knee.

When I came round after that ordeal, I found that my eyesight was rather worse than it had been before. I expect it was due to several things including nervous tension, but it had me worried I can tell you. I spent a full fortnight recuperating in hospital, but after the first week was up the nurses had me on my feet and walking about. However that was not enough for me; I felt I needed more exercise on my bad leg, so when no one was looking I used to slip down to the ground floor in the lift and with the aid of a couple of sticks I would walk round Fitzroy Square.

That strengthened my ability to go further afield and in the mornings I would be seen, or not seen, creeping out of the hospital to get over to Park Street near Marble Arch in order to have a consultation with the famous 'Tuck'. Tuck was Mr Bill Tucker, the 'bone' man who is a bit of a legend in horse racing circles as he has great skill in dealing with the problems that jockeys encounter with broken bones, pulled muscles and so on. Tuck was a very sympathetic man and he was the only medical man I felt I could talk to about my eyesight. While I was visiting him, Tuck suggested that I go and see a certain Harley Street specialist, which I eventually did.

I had a little bit of bad luck on the last of my clandestine trips to see Tuck because, after I had struggled on to the under-ground train to get me back to Warren Street, who should I sit next to but none other than the Matron of St Luke's. As Matrons do, she went absolutely spare, gave me a hell of a wigging and demanded to know where I had been. Well it isn't the best thing to tell the Matron of a hospital that is doing its best for you, that you have been off on your own seeing a specialist – even if it is for a different reason – so I said I had been out shopping. It seemed she was not at all pleased about my escapade.

Anyway, I took my deep worries about my faulty vision and disturbed mind to the neuro-surgeon recommended to me by Tuck. He was very high up in his profession, so when this man told me that my problems were perfectly normal for people who had suffered from bad concussion, and that as far as he was concerned I was as sane as the next man, I could have whooped with joy. However, my elation was short-lived. 'You will need about two years to fully recover from this,' he said in that matter-of-fact way medics have of knocking the mounting block from under your boot.

It was a very great shock to be told by so eminent an authority that it would be two years before I could really expect to get back into harness. Frankly, in my state of stupidity and shock I just did not believe him. All right, I thought, these experts are great men in their field, but can they be sure? It's only an opinion. I couldn't possibly wait that long. Pam was pregnant and still riding, trying desperately to keep the wolf from the door, but the yard looked doomed if I couldn't manage to earn anything for the next year, much less two.

I couldn't accept that I was not going to be fit again for so long and went to see all sorts of doctors to find out if any of them could be any more encouraging and tell me that it was all a mistake. Whatever the diagnosis from Harley Street did to me, it at least bucked Pam up at a time when she needed it very badly. She was very relieved to hear from a top specialist that her man was not actually destined for the loony bin and would perhaps, some time, somehow, pull through. As I have said, Pam is luckily much more phlegmatic than I and probably much more clear-thinking. Certainly she was at this particular time when she had to think for two of us, carry our child and ride big courses with all their potential danger. As for me, I was not at all happy with myself. I had lost the will to ride and I felt that what with my shoulder, my knee and my eyesight I was a spent force in the world of horses.

Despite this feeling, one very important thing happened while I was at St Luke's. It was odd that as I lay there in hospital with my leg strapped up, a new phase of my show jumping career started. It all began when Tony Elliott came to see me in hospital. I had sold him a horse a couple of years previously and he had been absolutely delighted with this animal and we had had contact on several occasions in the interim. Whenever we met we always talked horses and very little about his exotic fruit importing business which is Griffin and Brand's trade.

We had always talked about him having another horse and

he came in to see me when I was really and truly very low. I didn't tell him, but I was still having problems with my head and my eyes, and the back of my neck hurt, while my torn shoulder was still not really back to normal. I couldn't have any booze in the preacher's hospital, but Tony Elliott got me as near as he could to it by one evening coming in with a friend called Georgie Cottle who owns a few public houses in London, and Ronnie Jefferies who does the same thing, only more so! They came to try to cheer me up and to get me thinking towards horses again. At least Tony did because I remember him saying to me, 'I am going to buy you a horse. You've bought horses for me, now I'm going to buy you one.'

With that I sold him a half share in two horses, for whatever other faculties I might have lost, my feeling for business never deserted me. These two horses were called Shasta and Tiago, Tiago being none other than the same Union Jack on which I had had the horrendous fall in the previous year. Because horses have their official names swapped in a very abrupt manner, they often have a stable name so that the poor animals can get used to at least one of them. Both these horses were good, sound jumpers and so it was through them that Tony Elliott began in involvement with us that lasted right through until 1984.

All the time that we had Tony as an owner we felt a great debt to him. For instance he paid for two marvellous foreign holidays that we took in the middle of winter – it was impossible to take summer vacations in the height of the season. He stood behind us through thick and thin, and rarely wavered when we said that a particular horse was likely to make the grade and that he ought to buy it. Right through from 1976 until the spring of 1984 we rode all the major classes under the names of Griffin and Brand, or of Tony himself or of his wife Joyce. It is this memory of times past that makes the story that I have to tell at the end of this book so painful to me.

# 3 Jungle Bunny – and Other Problems

I was out of hospital by the end of September 1977 and so was able to go down to the Horse of the Year Show to see Vicky Baldock ride in the pony event for which she had qualified back in the summer. I don't quite remember now how well Vicky did, but I think she was in the money on Bombadillo. We stayed at the Crest Hotel and while we were there a fateful conversation took place between Pam and Freddie Welch, with whom I used to jump on the circuit.

He told her that he had this black horse that he had sold a couple of times and had got back again. It was, he said, a little bit on the difficult side, but Pam, unbeknown to me, went ahead and arranged that we would have Ganderbush and try him. We were pretty short of cash just then and so she arranged with Fred to pay a 'hunter' price for the horse and to pay him the balance if he proved to be as good as Freddie claimed.

So while I was still in a confused state due to drugs and the general after-effects of the accidents, I remember getting up one morning and Pam saying, 'We're going down to pick up this new horse I have bought you.' I was less than enthusiastic as I felt I had had enough of horses. I protested that I just wasn't interested, but she insisted and said forcefully, 'No arguments – you're coming.' So we hitched up the small horse box behind Pam's father's Volvo and drove off over to Freddie Welch's. Of course Pam had to drive because I was quite incapable at that time of co-ordinating mind, body and vision sufficiently to drive a car with a box behind it.

Now Freddie had his yard over at Turgis Green between Basingstoke and Reading and so we had to travel the horse a long way home. We found that whatever kind of a rogue Ganderbush was supposed to be, at least he was a good traveller. Which was just as well as Pam had a great deal on her plate just then, what with the worry of me and the lack of money. She was also heavy with our baby and all in all it was as tough for her as it was for me at that time. So it was lucky that the horse travelled well as we drove all those miles up the M4, through Watford and on to the A1 to get home. If he had been a real problem and had started to kick hell out of the box – as many horses might have done – I don't quite know how a pregnant woman and an incapacitated man could have coped.

The horse was put in the stable that faces the back door. Actually at home we have a covered brick-built annexe where we keep, for example, our great big freezer that makes the provisioning of our show jumping trips possible, and where we can shed our boots and coats when we come in out of the rain. Ganderbush was put in the stable which faces the arch leading out of the outhouse. So every morning the first thing I saw when I went out was that horse. It was all part of my cunning wife's plan to get me back to the saddle. Soon she was saying, 'When are you going to ride that horse?' Still I set my face against riding.

Ganderbush stayed in the yard, unridden, for a long time because I had no interest in riding him at all and Pam was now in no condition to ride even if she wanted to. Then she had to go into hospital with complications, and it was while she was away that I suddenly decided that I was going to sort this black blighter out. So, during the latter part of October, I first got on to Ganderbush and believe you me I had some problems. He was a little bit of a hot head – to put it mildly. He had very much a will of his own and was a stopper – full stop! He didn't want to do anything he was told, and believe me he was the best therapy I could have had. He had so many problems that I soon forgot my own. He was, and still is, such a difficult horse that even to this day I cannot walk into the stable and put a head-collar on him. He will either turn round and bite me or he will try to kick me.

Now it is an interesting side-light on the intelligence of horses that while I cannot get near him in the stable, the girl grooms he has had over the years have never had much problem. It must be because I am such a forceful rider and have tamed the horse and made him do as he is told. He says in effect: 'Take that, you bastard, for breaking my will to refuse and play up generally.'

Ganderbush is, of course, now Jungle Bunny. I coined the latter name in a fit of temper when the beast began bucking, as was his custom. I remember saying something like, 'I hate this bloody crazy jungle bunny,' and the name stuck.

On the top of the British Show Jumping Association's registration certificate for Jungle Bunny – which incidentally tells us that before he was Ganderbush he was Spectator II – there are two almost identical scribbled notes. One says 'Now to be Jungle Bunny!' and the other 'Now to be called Jungle Bunny?' The exclamation and question marks are mine, but I reckon they ought to have been there because I can remember being rung up by the Secretary General of the BSJA and told that because it was a politically sensitive name I might not be able to call the horse that. However, after the horse began to be so successful they dropped their objections and Jungle Bunny he has remained to this day; one of the greatest horses – if not the greatest – I have ever ridden.

With Pam in hospital I spent all my time with Jungle Bunny, and that is when my fight back began – the fight to get myself to where I had been before the big accident on Union Jack and to get to greater heights. He was a very difficult horse in the mouth because he had at one time broken his jaw and he wouldn't turn very well. But was he a powerful jumper? I'll say he was! And it was this ability over the fences that made me determined to tackle and beat the really big problem – that of getting him to the fences in the first place. Once you'd done that, then he would tackle whatever you put in front of him with confidence and power. Except, that is, for blue walls. He just hated blue walls and wouldn't go near them.

So although I couldn't really afford them, I was out buying every available wall that the fence-makers had to offer so that I could work Jungle Bunny over blue walls. I bought a viaduct wall, a semi-circular wall and an ordinary brick wall and made sure that they were supplied with one side painted blue. However I had to spend days, weeks and even months getting the horse to arrive at his fences cleanly so that he could have every chance of using the care and attention he displayed in jumping. Teaching a horse to jump fences which are at the heights and spreads of top international competitions requires precise timing. You have to know just how much ground your horse covers with each stride so that he can be perfectly placed for the final take-off stride. If you cannot do that as a rider, then you cannot hope to be a show jumper. Any sound horse can and will jump little fences up to about three feet high without needing an experienced jockey on his back. A big horse hardly needs to lift its body to clear three feet, because it tucks its feet up when going over the fence.

When the fences become over four feet high, however, things become different, and when they are between five and six feet high if you cannot ride your horse exactly into the take-off spot in front of the jump, and do it every time under all kinds of conditions, you might as well give up and do something else for a living. To bring Jungle Bunny to that degree of perfection and, at the same time, to re-educate my own body and mind, I had to choose the long hard road which in the end changed this very difficult horse into the great show jumper that he became.

By February I was gathering my strength and my confidence again. Jungle Bunny and I were clicking, and he was as much teaching me and making me feel better as I was teaching him. I suppose I feel towards Jungle Bunny as wounded soldiers do to the nurses who are instrumental in pulling them through. I developed a love relationship with that horse as my tortured mind and body became stronger day by day. I was pulling out of the nose-dive and I could see myself back in the show jumping game again.

Anyway other things were happening that helped me get back into business. I began to sound out the Middle East for customers and invited some from Khartoum, and I managed to sell no less than eight horses to the Sudanese government, together with their tack and associated equipment – rugs, rollers and the like. However, this was not the first contact I had had with the Sudanese government because in the previous November (1977) I had been approached to go to Khartoum to train Sudanese riders on a three-week course. Now I was not really fit to go, much less to ride, but the idea of three weeks in the sun with what it could do for the healing of my knee and shoulder persuaded me to accept.

So I went to Khartoum thinking I could well handle this assignment. I got to Khartoum at three in the morning, where I was picked up and whisked off to a hotel. I promise you that I have never felt more lonely in all my life than when I got into that hotel in a foreign land at that time in the morning when life is at its lowest ebb. It was not a particularly luxurious place and as far as I could see I was the only white man in the building. It gave me a real feeling of insecurity to realize that I was in an Arab country and that I was the only Englishman around.

I got no real sleep that night. I washed, shaved and freshened up generally, and was in the breakfast room by 5.30 a.m. There I had the luck to discover another white person, but he was just on his way back to England. However birds of a feather flock together and we had a long chat and he put me wise on a whole host of things which I should and shouldn't do when trying to do business in that part of the world. I shall never see that chap again – I have no idea what his name was – but I shall always be eternally grateful to him for his advice, without which I am sure I would never have pulled off the deal that I did manage to clinch.

It was when I was there that I got this order for eight horses, including four Welsh pony mares and a stallion. In the meantime I telexed back to Pam what was required and she set about trying to find the animals. She found the necessary stock and I invited my Sudanese contacts to come over to the Olympia Show that December. I thought that they would really profit from seeing the top jumpers performing in these ideal surroundings. They were, not unnaturally, pretty ignorant of the show jumping world as it is in Europe. In fact I can illustrate how little progress they had made out there by revealing that when I went to Khartoum they did not have one show jumping fence.

So I managed to persuade the boss of the federation out there to buy some wood and get some carpenters together so they could knock up a set of twelve to fourteen fences. The resulting fences might not have been exactly up to BSJA standard, but they were perfectly adequate and were the first coloured jumps that most of the Sudanese had seen.

In the end I needn't have been so worried about being the only white man on the place, for they treated me extremely well and I behaved in a way that pleased them as a result of the advice of my unknown instructor. In fact they treated me better than well – they almost worshipped me as a god. When you have a skill that others want and have never had the chance of obtaining, they take whatever you say as absolute gospel. So I was a much happier person at the end of the three weeks than at the beginning. I had been able to cope with the food by the expedient of living on fish – which my hotel friend had said was the safest thing to eat. My hosts had taken me out almost every night when we were not working, and we had had a very good time even if I perhaps did not see more than three or four other Europeans all the time I was there.

Nevertheless, I had to work hard for my money. We started at about 5.30 a.m. and worked through until about 8.00 a.m. when it began to get unbearably hot. The local custom is to have a siesta from about 8.30 a.m. right through until about 4.00 in the afternoon. Then we would train again from 4 p.m. until 6.00 p.m.

Now this was all very well, but I was getting a bit fed up with such short sessions and I knew I was just not getting enough time with my pupils for them to really benefit in three short weeks. So I decided we'd have to work after dark and would need some lights. So the little, or maybe great, god spoke, and by next evening the organizers had managed to erect a lighting system in and around the clubhouse so that I could give evening lectures as well as some videos I had brought with me. In this way I was able to further the education of the youngsters I was training.

We now changed to an early morning session that lasted from 6.00 until 9.30, followed by an evening session that started at 4.00 and went on sometimes well after dark. Sometimes we didn't stop before 10.00 or 11.00, which may not have been in accordance with local customs but it certainly helped the training. I was not only training show jumpers; I also had a load of kids who needed to be introduced to every kind of gymkhana race that I could remember. I not only introduced those Sudanese youngsters to all the games in the Pony Club book, but I made up a lot more on the spur of the moment.

My gymkhana races were not all that orthodox, because they nearly always contained a jump of some description which they never do over here. I wanted to get these kids jumping because my brief was to train as many as possible to jump. Of course they had never jumped before and any riding instructors will throw up their hands in despair if asked to train children to jump in a couple of weeks, which is all I had. So I decided that while they played at gymkhana, which was much more in the Arab tradition, they could also play at jumping.

Those kids really appreciated what I tried to do for them because, on my birthday, they gave me a party with even a birthday cake. As well as that, one of the adults I taught presented me with three solid silver ashtrays depicting the last three reigning monarchs of the Sudan. Even more valuable than these was the present of a big horse as well as gifts of handbags for my wife and other things made in the local Sudanese tradition.

As soon as I got back to England Pam again had complications and had to go back into hospital temporarily. While she was away, the Sudanese whom I had invited arrived over here and I took them to the Olympia Show, which they really enjoyed, although I don't know how much of it they fully understood. We are so used to the kind of jumping competitions that have developed over here that we tend to forget that others from foreign lands have not had our experience or background. The show jumping scene in the Middle East is developing apace and they have plenty of money to buy good horses. However it takes years to train riders and that is what is lacking in places like the Sudan.

As well as the horses which I sold them, they went to Newmarket and bought a string of racehorses through Dr MacEnery, a very well-known veterinary surgeon who is now a bloodstock agent. Between us we managed to get enough horses of one kind and another to fill a plane which flew them off to Khartoum.

It was now all go for me. I had worked hard at getting fit and my knee was mended, while my shoulder, which had taken so long to heal, was at last working. Along with these improvements my eyesight was also much more reliable. It wasn't a hundred per cent right but it was much, much better. I was no longer losing vision as I had been – sometimes it went a little hazy, but that was all. In the interim I had got my doctor to find me a tranquillizer that would quieten the pain in the back of my neck only and nothing more.

I gave Jungle Bunny a preliminary outing before Christmas at Mill Lodge, which is a riding establishment near Cambridge, and he got a fifth in a minor class, so I won £5 – the first money I ever won on him.

Christmas came and went, and with Pam at home we had a happy family Christmas, but it was also a very hard-working time. I was out every available minute working on Jungle Bunny and trying to knock sense into his head. While everyone else was putting their feet up round the fire and downing the Christmas cheer, I was out riding in the cold and wet to get the best chance I could of bringing off some kind of win in the New Year's events at Mill Lodge.

I was pretty happy with the Jungle Bunny partnership by now and of course I expected to win on him. However my crazy Jungle Bunny had other ideas. He was quite OK in the first clear round event until we got to the blue wall. You will remember I had worked so hard on that bogy fence at home, but he nevertheless refused to jump it. I was desperately disappointed as I thought we had broken the jinx. The next event was a Gambler's Stakes. In this event each fence has a number somewhere between ten and 120 and the wall was 100. I deliberately left it until last because in this event you can jump the fences in any order, but the toughest fences have the highest numbers. The rider who gets the highest number of points in the allotted time wins. As I came up to the wall we were winning – we had more points than anyone at that stage.

Once again Jungle Bunny did not want to know about jumping that wall, but as you get two tries at each fence I turned him round and forced him to jump it. He was even then such a great performer that despite that stop we still finished eighth. It was my first real win with the horse who was to become my mainstay for the next few years.

Jungle Bunny had shown what potential he had, while I had,

after all, got him over the bogy fence. So I was fired that late winter and early spring to work very very hard on the horse so as to get him fit for the real season that was to come. I took him around all the smaller shows to give him the mileage on the clock that is an absolute necessity for a top jumper. He has to have seen whatever the course-builders can throw at him and to forge on regardless of blue walls, vertical uprights or massive parallels stuffed with brush. Each of these forms of fence and others like triple bars, which slope up in the direction of jumping, has to be tackled differently and each one demands that the horse be placed exactly where he has the best possible chance of making a clean take-off and so clearing the fence.

That kind of precision entails not only jumping many fences in all sorts of different combinations, but even more careful work on the ground so that he becomes so tuned to your aids as to shorten or lengthen his stride instantly when asked. Horse and rider have to become one – each responding to the other's thoughts and feelings as if they were joined by some invisible cord of understanding. The horse has to become a sort of robot, but one which thinks for itself when the need arises.

The really great horses are ones which not only have the ability to jump carefully and cleanly, but have another ingredient in their make-up – they have to be what, for want of a better word, we would call 'characters'. Jungle Bunny, I knew, was a character. It is becoming almost commonplace to see outstanding show jumping horses described as 'difficult' in their early days. Now that I was making some progress with Jungle Bunny I was quite pleased that he'd had an awful reputation as a difficult horse before I got him. There was something special about him and I was determined that spring to show the world that Lionel Dunning was not yet dead and that he could still bring out the best in a horse, even one with a bad reputation, and hone it to take on the best in the world.

Meanwhile there were two strokes of misfortune in the Dunnings' yard at that time. You will remember I told you of the two horses in which I had sold half-shares to Tony Elliott, namely Shasta and Union Jack. Both of them were lost to us that spring in tragic circumstances. I had taken Shasta to Millfields, which is one of the indoor arenas on the winter jumping circuit near Newmarket. They had a very uneven collecting ring there in those days, and the poor horse pulled a tendon. Despite all our efforts the damned leg never did come sound and eventually he had to be sold for a small sum as a hack.

Then, in February, Union Jack did a stupid thing. He was left in the accommodation yard with a herd of bullocks. Someone had left a load of hay outside the gate ready to feed in the morning. Union Jack couldn't wait that long and put his foot through the gate to try to paw the hay in towards him so that he could get to it; but he got his foot stuck in the gate and all night long he pulled and pulled to free his trapped leg. He so lacerated his leg that by morning it was cut right through to the bone and it was the most ghastly mess you ever saw. It was an accident most likely to induce acute tetanus infection. When the vet came he recommended that the poor horse be put down at once as there was no chance of it recovering.

Now I felt pretty bad about this. It was one thing to lose one of the Elliott horses, but to have lost both of them and in such a short space of time was almost unbelievable. Still, luckily, there was the up-and-coming Jungle Bunny. He had no form except for some minor places in a few small classes, but even so I had enough faith in his potential to put him into the Griffin and Brand name. Prior to this I had asked Mr Elliott whether he wanted to be connected with Jungle Bunny, but he was just not convinced of the horse's worthiness and didn't want to know. So I was sticking my neck right out in an attempt to keep alive what looked like being the end of a useful partnership.

Now that Pam was in the throes of having Robert and couldn't earn anything at shows, and I had only just begun to get back to show jumping and had not yet won anything worth having, we were in a bad way for funds. If you don't keep horses yourself then you can have no idea how much it takes to keep a show jumping yard going. If you do, then you will have some inkling of what we were up against.

You cannot hope to be a successful show jumper if you do not have at least three top-grade horses that you can call on when required. The best-known and highly successful names like David Broome, Harvey Smith, Alwin Schockemöhle and Eddie

Macken got to the top not only by virtue of a great ability to train and ride the horses they had, but also by having a string of really good horses to choose from. In the spring of 1978 the Dunning family had no chance of competing in this highest league if for no other reason than that they did not have the horses to back up their efforts. This was why I saw Jungle Bunny as a light at the end of the very long and horrible tunnel that I had been crawling through for the last couple of years. I was not yet out into the light of day, but there was hope.

Pam meanwhile gave birth to Robert on Friday 13 February by caesarian; our son was a good ten pounds at birth and there was no way he was going to struggle into the world through normal channels. So despite all she'd been through Pam had to face the trauma of the operation and the post-caesarian recuperation.

Hardly had I seen our new baby than I had to go back to the Sudan. Well perhaps I could have said no, but we needed the money badly and the Sudanese had been pestering me to go back for months – ever since I got back from the first trip. This time things were different. Now I could actually ride and show them what I wanted them to do.

However tough I think I am, I reckon Pam is tougher still. After the birth of Robert she was back in the saddle and working on her lost muscles the moment she felt able to do so. I suppose both of us felt a bit desperate at that time. We were obviously glad to have a baby son, but it had badly interrupted Pam's jumping programme and as her winnings are a major part of our income there were more than the normal pressures on her to get back into harness.

Although, when babies come along, it is tough on mothers who have to have them, that does not stop the husband being invited out to celebrate the new arrival! On the Saturday evening after Robert's birth a great friend of mine, Robert Bray, asked me over for a celebration. It was snowing that evening and Pam's father loaned me his car to go to the Brays' party. He did this because at the time I was driving a Triumph Pi – one of the earlier fuel injection cars – and I had been known to go just a weeny bit fast in it. Pam's father's car was a more sedate Volvo, and so I suppose my father-in-law, not wanting

Jumping at Burley, in the New Forest, at the age of twelve. The promise of future success is already evident in the sensitive rein-contact with Just Jane.

First birthday in 1939. War had broken out, but babies still had something to laugh about.

Riding my brilliant pony Nipper to victory at the Brighton Horse Show in 1953.

Lyndhurst High Street in the 1940s. The riding school where I first learned to ride was round the corner to the right off the Cadnam Road.

An historic picture. David Kingsley of Everest Double Glazing, show jumping's leading sponsors, presents the shield to the winner of the first class that Everest ever sponsored – at the South of England Show in 1969. The horse is George Forbes's Strathdon.

At the 1972 Horse of the Year Show, at Wembley, Chane Link nuzzles up to the trophy for the Dick Turpin Stakes, in which we beat Alwin Schockemöhle, on Weiler, into second place.

The best of pals. With Sporting Award and David Broome and his Ballywillwill at the Butlins Horse Show at Bognor Regis in 1974.

Happy faces at Laxenburg in 1974, after the team had come second to Germany by just half a point. Pam is nearest the camera on Sugar Plum, I am on Tuffet, Alison Dawes (*née* Westwood) is on Tuxedo, while Liz Edgar (*née* Broome) is on Everest Make Do.

Winning the Finmere Show's major class – the William Hill Open – on
Jungle Bunny. We won this event three years running.

Fanny Hill, one of my great horses, winning the Six Bar Jumping competition at the Royal Windsor in 1974. The top rail is near seven feet.

Jumping on the snow and ice at Davos called for special studs. Here I am applying my 'secret weapon' of water-pump grease to the hoofs of Harry Seymour's grey mare Lesia.

Calgary, 1979. I have Jungle Bunny, Pam has Roscoe, and between us is our long-time owner Tony Elliott.

The family man, at home with Pam and our son Robert.

to see his daughter widowed and his new grandson fatherless, imagined that I would drive more carefully in his car than in my own.

Well it was a great evening but then some funny things happened. We toasted the boy and his mother, and then the proud father, and then the mother, and then the son again and so on until I suppose I was just a little the worse for wear. It was then that I lost the keys to my father-in-law's car as I prepared unsteadily to come home in the early hours of Sunday morning.

I went to the coat-rack in the hall and felt in the pocket of the Crombie coat I had come in – no keys! I felt in the other pocket – nothing. Then I went a bit frantic and soon the whole household was in an uproar searching high and low, but they were nowhere to be found. It wasn't until Robert went to put on his own Crombie coat to help me look in the Volvo in case the keys were there that we discovered that I had his Crombie coat and he had mine.

So having now found the keys I set off for home in the snow. I don't remember much about that trip except that it was snowing quite hard and the roads were slippery, so I did in fact go pretty slowly – at least I think I did. Anyway I got home and as far as I was aware I put the car away and went to bed. I didn't think I was all that far gone because I had the sense to take a couple of Alka Seltzers before I dropped off to help me sober up.

The next thing I knew I was awake and the dawn was just breaking, but then I realized that I was in bed with my shoes on. What had I done? I leaped out of bed and went downstairs. The whole house was a blaze of light. It seemed that almost every light was on. And what was that in the middle of the kitchen table? It was my rolled-up pyjamas which I had taken to Robert's in case they asked me to stay the night.

The next thought was 'Where is the car?' So I went out and looked in the yard – no car. Then I looked in father-in-law's drive – no car. At that point I really did begin to worry. If I had no recollection of bringing in my pyjamas and putting them on the table and, if I could get into bed with my shoes on, I was thinking, God knows where the car is. I ran out to the front and looked into the road. There, sure enough, was the car. It was parked in the road, but with the driver's door open, the engine still running and the headlamps full on.

Now our village in Lincolnshire is a quiet little place, but it was only the fact that it was the early hours of the morning, and a snowy one at that, which had prevented me creating a major obstruction in the High Street or, worse, a nasty accident. However the sudden realization that any Tom, Dick or Harry could have come along, jumped into a ready-to-run Volvo and driven it off without trace sobered me up at a very rapid rate. Luckily the wind had blown from the passenger door side and so not too much snow had collected in the car and I was able to brush it out and quietly get the car up on the hard-standing in front of our two houses, which are next door to one another.

As it was, when father-in-law came in to see me that morning he had some idea that my homecoming had been a little peculiar to say the least because of course he could see the tyre marks in the snow and the rather strange manoeuvres I had undertaken to get the car to where it now stood. He assumed I had had a good night, but I didn't have the courage to explain that for a couple of hours or more his car had been sitting in the High Street just waiting for some bright person to come and drive it away or, failing that, take off the driver's door as they skidded past in the snow. It was also lucky that Pam was in hospital because I was able to get the bed sheets, soiled by my outdoor shoes, laundered before she came home!

As it was she was not too pleased with me, but for another reason.

I had already upset Pam a couple of days earlier when, trying to be a dutiful father-to-be, I had gone to visit her in hospital just before the caesarian, and then waved her goodbye temporarily while I slipped out for a meal before coming back to see her again. It was not a very marvellous meal, but I enjoyed it, and anyway with Pam away I wasn't eating too well at home on my own. I told her all about my meal, thinking she would be happy to know that her man was not suffering from starvation while she was unable to look after him. What I didn't consider was that because of the impending operation poor Pam had been without food for the last twelve hours while I had been out feeding the inner man. I have never been allowed to forget that while she starved I regaled her with a long and mouth-watering list of what I had just had for supper.

I also forgot that maybe a mother too would like to toast her baby's health in a drop of champers. I didn't think about that in the aftermath of my night on the tiles, but ever since then Pam has cracked a bottle of champagne on the night of Robert's birthday, and while she may share a glass with our nanny, Kate, she never, ever, invites me to the party – just to remind me, I suppose.

# 4  Childhood Days

Now I look back on it, there is no doubt about it – even as a youngster I was a little devil. I was born just before the Second World War near Southampton and so I grew up under wartime conditions. Of course as kids we did not understand that things were really any different from normal, except from being frightened by the air-raids on Southampton. I recall very little about that time, but I do remember, when I was four, being sent to the local greengrocer's by my mother to buy some potatoes. So off I went clutching a sixpence in my hand – you could get a goodly number of potatoes for that in those days.

When I got to the shop there was the inevitable queue. I believe the British got through the war without fighting amongst themselves because they were so disciplined in a queue. You queued for everything from beef to bullseyes, but as a four-year-old I didn't know anything about that. So I marched up to the head of the queue and thrust my sixpence at the lady shopkeeper. She looked at me sternly and ordered me to the back of the queue to await my turn.

This treatment did not go down well with me at all. In fact it made me quite angry. The end of the queue was by the door and instead of joining it I slipped out, locked the door behind me, took the key and dropped it down the first drain I came across. Then I ran home to carry on playing and forgot all about it until my mother came to ask what I had done with the potatoes. I must have said something like, 'Oh sorry Mum, they didn't have any.'

In the meantime down at the shop, which was a lock-up with only one door, the people imprisoned within were attracting the attention of passers-by with messages smeared on the window and cries for help. I'm told that someone had to send for the fire brigade to break down the door and let everyone out.

Now that is the kind of kid I was as I grew up living over my father's butcher's shop in Totton. Totton is about the last western outpost of Southampton as you cross the bridge over the estuary of the River Test where it flows into Southampton Water, on the very edge of the New Forest – a fact that was to have a great bearing my future life.

Back in the thirties and early forties Totton was quite a small place, but like so many of the little towns and villages that lay inland from the frequently bombed ports of Southampton and Portsmouth it grew as people were forced to move out of the town centres.

I remember my first school was a very small private establishment run by a lady in the Ringwood Road in the front room of her bungalow. My parents were not fantastically rich, but they had enough to ensure that I was going to get a 'good' education at whatever private school would take me. So at the age of five I found myself behind a desk in this school room and asked to sit still for two whole hours.

The first day at school is pretty bad for most kids, but it was purgatory for me. I had always been free to play in the yard behind the shop, and while I had very few playmates – mainly because my parents frowned on small boys coming into their yard – at least it had been the freedom I loved. Now they were asking me to do the impossible – sit still and keep quiet.

I had a desk at the back of the room and being bored I looked around to see what ways there were of escaping. They had big sash windows in this bungalow and the bottom was partly open so when the schoolmistress's back was turned I pushed up the window and was gone. She couldn't have seen me do it or even have been aware that I had gone until it was too late.

However I had a problem – I didn't know the way home. Still I must have been a resourceful kid because I knew the railway line ran past home and there was a railway line running past the back of the bungalow. Luckily it was the same railway line and I set off in the right direction, running alongside the track until I reached our house. My mother and father were not at all pleased about that, but it was just the first of a long series of skirmishes during my schooldays.

When I was seven the war ended and they sent me to another private school at Bitterne. Now Bitterne is on the other side of

Southampton, and even after two changes of bus I still had to walk three miles to the school. So I had a very long day starting from home at 7.30 in the morning and often not getting home until 6 o'clock in the evening.

I hated that school, the drudgery of the journey and the strictness of the masters. My father did not help because every time we went to a new school and had an interview with a headmaster my dad would put me in his bad books by saying something like, 'Now if this boy does anything that warrants a good leathering then you have my express permission to give it to him.' So I was branded a bad lot before I even set foot in the school. Not that I expect I did much to reverse that idea because as I disliked school I just went on rebelling in my own little way although I must have done something very bad there as my parents were asked to take me away.

My mother had been brought up in a convent and was pretty strict. Perhaps this added to my feelings in those early days that my parents did not understand me or give me the real love I craved and needed. As I see it now, my constant rebellion was probably the result of the strictness of my parents – I felt that the world was against me. Not that the rest of the family helped, as my cousins (my father had two brothers and three sisters) used to keep on ribbing me because I went to a 'posh' school, whereas they only went to State schools.

You can imagine the furore when little Lionel had been expelled, and it only added to the gulf between my parents and me. An even bigger factor was that my brother Malcolm was born when I was eight; obviously parents dote on babies, so I felt rejected and pushed out. Those early experiences have never quite left me and, unfortunately, my brother and I have never been as close as some brothers are. If all this sounds like a catalogue of woe and 'poor me', I can only say that these were the factors that made me feel this way and may help you to understand my future life.

After the terrible disgrace of being expelled from the school at Bitterne I suppose my parents thought that they were wasting money on my education and so I went to the Ringwood Road Primary School. Even the first day I was in trouble and found myself waiting at the bottom of the stairs to be summoned to the headmaster's room. Now my father used to supply the meat to the kitchens at that school and he was, to me, more of a threat than the headmaster. So, when I looked out of the front entrance of the school and saw my father's van driving in with the meat, I was terrified. I had only been there five minutes and already I was in trouble. So I looked around for an avenue of escape. There it was! A broom cupboard – and little did my dad know who was inside it as he carried in the meat within feet of where I was hiding. I had several other occasions to use that broom cupboard in the following couple of years.

By the time I was ten I was doing a bit better at school and it was at this time that I began to hanker after a pony. In fact, looking back on it, I must have driven my parents half mad with the way I went on about this wretched pony. However, it was, as they pointed out, impossible to keep a pony in the yard of a butcher's shop in the middle of Totton, but they saw I was determined to start riding and so they let me go to a riding school.

Now I was lucky to have been born and brought up so close to the New Forest because it is the most marvellous riding country and only a short bus ride brought me to a little riding school in Lyndhurst. Lyndhurst is the 'capital' of the New Forest and is often called the 'Gateway to the Forest'. Today it is absolutely chock-a-block with visitors who come in droves to picnic, caravan and camp in its beautiful surroundings. In those days, however, it was still quite a sleepy little market town and there were no one-way streets to confuse the motorist as there are today.

Perhaps one of the most delightful aspects of the Forest is the way the wild, open areas lap the shorelines of little towns and villages like Lyndhurst. Bridleways meander almost unnoticed between the cottages and lead to the rides and open spaces between the enclosures. It was not very far to the open forest, but the riding school was right in the middle of Lyndhurst on the Cadnam Road and its site is now occupied by shops. However, just recently I found an old guidebook that showed what the High Street looked like in 1939 and you could almost see our riding school, so perhaps the horse pictured being ridden down the almost deserted street, leading a mare and her foal, was one of ours. Just across the High Street from the site of the stables is St Michael's churchyard, which contains the grave of a Mrs Hargreaves, who was the 'Alice' of *Alice in Wonderland* and who once lived in Lyndhurst.

There was of course no indoor school, as is found in many riding schools today, but to me it was a magic place, with the ponies and horses looking over their rather ramshackle stable doors. However, it was a very wet yard when I arrived, as it was raining, and it didn't stop raining all that afternoon when I should have been having my first hack out on a lead rein on to the tracks and bridleways of the New Forest.

I recall vividly my intense disappointment as I sat miserably watching the rain while my father got from Mr Paterson, the man who ran the school, the details of when and how I was going to be taught to ride. However to an eager boy the idea of jam tomorrow is not good enough, but at least I did get to meet some ponies including one I was destined to see more of in the future. It was a small grey pony called Silver Fish, but the pony on which I was going to start learning was a dun called Sandy.

So while I didn't get a ride that first soggy day there were plenty of days to come and the whole of that first wonderful riding summer passed far too quickly for me. I was given lessons on Sandy by Mr Paterson who first of all made sure I could not bomb off by keeping me secure with a lead rein. For those who do not know much about riding and have never had any lessons let me explain that it is common practice, when taking beginners out on the open tracks and roads, to attach a lead rope to the bridle of the newcomer's pony or horse so that if it should decide to take off it can immediately be restrained by the instructor. This way the beginner feels more secure and can concentrate on learning to balance and absorb the new and often uncomfortable motion of the horse or pony. It also prevents some nasty accidents. If you ever go to a small riding school – or a big one for that matter – and they start taking you or your children out in the open without being on a lead rein, then you should insist that they do so. It may seem awfully grand and advanced to start riding on your own without restraint, but it is also a wonderful way to put people off riding for ever. To start on a lead rein is not cissy – in some of the most advanced riding academies in the world their pupils do not come off the lead rein before a year or more is up.

So I became pony mad. At weekends in term-time and most of the time during the holidays I was off to Lyndhurst to ride. By this time I had graduated to Silver Fish, and when winter came Mr Paterson asked me if I'd like to go hunting. My answer to that was obvious and so, one exciting day, there I was on Silver Fish, well secured by a lead rein to Mr Paterson and done up in my hunting garb.

The hunt was starting from Swan Green which is just outside Lyndhurst on the Christchurch Road, and so it was an easy hack from the stables to the meet. I don't remember everything about that day, but I well recall the Master – Major Sir George Llewellyn Tapps-Gervis-Meyrick. I was just eleven, but I was privileged to see possibly the last of the great country squires attired in his hunting pink (it's another of the oddities of the horse world that hunting pink is actually red) and giving tongue to his fog-horn voice. That he could dominate this elegant collection of gentlemen and ladies, each of whom I imagined was someone of importance, struck awe into me. However I was absolutely new to the hunting field and while Mr Paterson had gone out of his way to instruct me in the etiquette and mystique of the hunt, most of what he had told me was forgotten in the excitement of the moment.

I was starting my hunting career in Rhinefield, a very fashionable place – in fact a Royal place, for Rhinefield House is built on the site of William the Conqueror's hunting lodge. The area called Rhinefield Walk lies south of where we met, and we were led there by the hounds. Part of it consists of a great swathe of green turf that runs westwards from Brock-enhurst and spreads either side of a depression or 'rhine' where once an ancient stream flowed. Even today it can get very soggy along the rhines of the Rhinefield. It is cropped close and the hovering clumps of gorse and broom are held at bay by the herds of half-wild ponies that are such an attractive feature of the area. Away from the Rhinefield there are sandy and gravelly rides up through the trees – wonderful cover for foxes.

It was, I found, fantastic fun to go hunting, because Silver

Fish was a real little goer and galloped alongside Mr Paterson's mount at breath-taking speed every time the hounds gave tongue and we went off in pursuit. So much so that at one point Mr Paterson lost the lead rein and away went Silver Fish at a wild gallop, with me hanging on for dear life.

Now one of the most awful crimes in hunting is to ride ahead of the Master, but that is what I did! I couldn't do anything to stop Silver Fish carting me past the field, past the Field Master, who was also the Master's wife, and then there I was careering past the great man himself. It is probably as well that I cannot remember exactly which obscenities roared from the old man as this small boy overtook him to end up among the hounds.

I eventually came to rest on a mossy bank as the hounds turned one way and my pony turned the other, throwing me to the ground. Then I got the most tremendous wigging from Sir George on the do's and don'ts of hunting, and I couldn't have pleased Mr Paterson either because the incident spoiled his day's hunting as he was instructed to take this unruly boy home. However he couldn't say too much to me as it was his fault that he let go of the lead rein in the first place, and once you get a fresh pony in the wide open spaces with all the excitement of the hunt inside him nothing is going to hold him back.

The following spring the riding school was forced to close down, as it was losing money, and all the ponies and horses came up for sale. It seemed like the end of the world to me, as I had become really attached to Silver Fish and couldn't think of him being sold. I badgered and badgered my father to buy me the pony, knowing full well that if I didn't get him to agree soon my precious Silver Fish would be sold. Luckily I also had an ally in the shape of my grandfather who, having been around horses all his life, was able to understand my distress.

So it was that I set off, with my father and grandfather, to see if we could buy Silver Fish. It was awful for me and I still remember how I felt: the journey seemed to take hours, and with every moment that passed I could imagine my pony being sold to someone else. But I needn't have worried – Silver Fish was still there and because of my grandfather's knowledge of horses he could see at once that my pony was a real 'good un' (as they say down in Hampshire). So my father took his word for it and after a bit of haggling I got Silver Fish with saddle and bridle for £55.

Every kid who has ever wanted a pony and has managed to get one knows the intense feeling of joy that comes over you when the magic day dawns and somehow the impossible dream comes true. I felt like that, and it is one of the moments of my life that I treasure above all others. The generosity of my parents in buying me Silver Fish affected me deeply. I often felt that perhaps they didn't care much about me and yet here they were paying out a lot of money on a pony for *me*. So I did something about it.

In those days pocket money was not what it is today and I had half-a-crown a week. But that autumn and up to Christmas I saved my pocket money religiously and bought my mother and father a surprise present. I had seen an old hunting horn in an antique shop in Lyndhurst and I was determined to buy it for them for Christmas. It was one of those with a slight curve and looked very elegant. Unbeknown to them I wrapped up the precious gift and put it in the car with the other presents. We were going to Grandma and Grandpa Dunning for Christmas, as we always did up until I was eleven.

It was going to be great, I thought, to see my Mum's and Dad's faces when they saw what I had saved so hard to get them, but it was not to be. When on our way to my grandparents' we parked outside a friend's house and while we were inside some despicable person, or persons, stole all the Christmas presents. So, the joy of having a pony was followed by this – one of the greatest disappointments of my life – and we had a very lean Christmas that year with no presents. However, when I told them what I had bought for them they knew how grateful I was, and perhaps it made up for when I was a naughty, inattentive schoolboy.

Most kids get into scrapes at school, and you already know how I seemed to invite trouble. However, now I look back to those days I can see that I deserved all I got because I did some pretty naughty things, some of which I remember very well indeed. This is possibly because they were afterwards impressed on my backside by the headmaster's cane.

At one of the schools I went to we had a history teacher called Miss Churchwood. History as taught in many schools in those days was a pretty boring subject and I just didn't really pay attention. So Miss Churchwood and I did not get on – in fact she always seemed to be picking on me.

So I planned to get my own back. There was a girl in the class called Eileen, whom I was rather sweet on, and I can see this girl now in her tight-fitting yellow dress so she must have made an impression on me. However, she is only incidental to the story, being merely the accomplice who stole the cushion that protected Miss Churchwood's posterior from the ravages of the hard wooden chairs that the school authorities supplied for their teachers.

I had found the skin of a hedgehog that had, like so many of these unfortunate creatures, been squashed by passing traffic. It was old and didn't smell, but it still had a good collection of prickly spines. So Eileen undid the end of the cushion while I, and a few others who were only too happy to help, stuffed the poor old hedgehog skin into the cushion. Then the obliging Eileen sewed it up again, and just before she arrived for a lesson we slipped the cushion back on to Miss Churchwood's chair.

You can imagine what happened when the poor unfortunate lady went to sit down. She literally jumped a foot into the air with a piercing 'Ow!' I cannot remember how they knew it was me, but maybe I couldn't contain my mirth or something. Anyway, there I was up before the Head again and this time it was maximum punishment which was six strokes on each hand and six on the bottom. Yet somehow punishment like this did nothing to deter me from my life of petty 'crime'.

Like the time we dyed the girls blue. I expect you remember your PT teachers (or PE teachers as they are called now). We had two, one for the boys and one for the girls. The boys' was a Mr Jones, nicknamed 'Spike' after the band called Spike Jones and his City Slickers, who were up-and-coming at the time. He was a real tough guy who boxed and was something of a hero to us boys. The girls' PT teacher also took us for maths – a subject

I didn't get on too well with and one morning she really gave me a dressing down over some sum or other I couldn't do. It must have made me really mad because I vowed I'd get even with her.

It was PT first lesson next morning and we always had to have a shower after the lesson. So I got into school quite early that morning armed with a bottle of blue dye that I had found by rummaging through my mother's bathroom cupboard. With the aid of a couple of friends I managed to tip the whole of the bottle of dye into the tank that supplied the girls' showers.

This time I did not get caught, but I supposed I deserved to, as the girls all got covered in blue dye and, while it wasn't at all fair on the poor girls, it was rather a cheeky way of getting back at that teacher.

Getting back to my pony, despite what my dad had said earlier there now seemed to be room to build a stable for Silver Fish out behind the shop. It was a makeshift affair and the surroundings were, as I know now, quite unsuitable for keeping a pony, but there it was, I had my pony and this was the only place where we could keep him. And I really must have touched my father's soft spot with my stolen Christmas present, because every evening he would cycle miles with me on the lead rein as I rode Silver Fish, who I now realize was too strong and active for me at the time. After all, I had only had a year's lessons and that does not equip you with enough horse sense to handle an active bundle of flesh, bone and muscle who is being kept all day in an unsuitable stable in a butcher's yard.

However things were changing, and my maternal grandmother owned a house up on the Salisbury Road, almost opposite where my other grandparents lived. This became vacant and we moved there. It had a large garden, but you cannot keep a pony on less than about half an acre if it is to do well. So, while Silver Fish had his stable in the garden, it was not long before my father bought a little field up the way where the pony could be kept in more suitable conditions and where I could ride him. Even so, at this time much of my riding was on the roads, and while Silver Fish was a bit 'hot', as they say in horse circles, he was always bomb-proof on the road. How much of that was due to my father's marathons with me on the lead rein I don't know, but I can honestly say that I never had any real trouble with my pride and joy when riding on the roads.

At about this time I struck up a friendship with David Stanmore, the son of a farmer who owned a farm at the back of our house. David also became a show jumper, but gave it up for racing and one year he was the leading amateur jockey over fences. Anyway we spent most of our spare time practising gymkhana races.

Soon all this practising had to be put to the test and so off we used to go to shows. There was no horse box to take us so we had to hack to whatever local shows there were and sometimes we would go as far afield as Romsey which was a ride of several miles up along the valley of the Blackwater and Test. You could see, across the Test, the great pile of Broadlands House rising amongst the trees. Broadlands is where Earl Mountbatten lived, and where Prince Charles and Princess Diana stayed for the first part of their honeymoon. Not that connections with Royalty would have made any difference to us two boys. We were too keen on going to shows and leading double lives.

It cost half-a-crown to enter for the gymkhana races and while one of us went to enter the other one would give pony rides at sixpence a go. Giving five rides earned us the price of one set of races and so our gymkhana outings cost us hardly anything and were super fun. Anyway we began to get expert and were always walking away with the rosettes. It is funny now I look back on it, but whatever I did I couldn't make Silver Fish jump. He just didn't seem to want to and I didn't at that time know how to train him to jump and develop his potential. So it was all the fun of the gymkhana for us, but we each had our specialities. I was the expert at the bending race as well as the musical sacks, while David excelled at the can race and the egg and spoon race.

One day my father hired a horse box and we went all the way to Bransgore on the other side of the New Forest, down towards Christchurch. We had become such expert gymkhana protagonists that we came back from that outing no less than £12 in pocket. My father, being a business man, saw the potential in that and it turned him from a cricket fanatic into a horse show fanatic overnight.

I had been on at him for ages about the fact that Silver Fish was a lovely pony, but that he wouldn't jump, which was what I wanted. I kept on about jumping until one day I was bought a mare called Just Jane and then another called Melody so that I could start to jump. We now had more stables in the garden, as I was not going to part with my precious Silver Fish, and at the same time David's father bought him a jumping pony called Linda.

I had quite a bit of success with Melody and you might say that it was on her that my show jumping career started. However, Melody was not the finest piece of horse flesh and so later Dad bought me another horse called Blue Mink.

I gained a lot of experience on Blue Mink, who came from the Benenden Riding Establishment in Kent and had been ridden by a girl called Judith Kendall in the days before I had him. However the pony was trained by the famous Snowey Mitcherson, whom I mention elsewhere. This is when he was head trainer and instructor at Benenden. I was always round the local shows with Blue Mink and my old love Silver Fish. I used to ride Blue Mink in the jumping events and then transfer to Silver Fish when it came to the gymkhana games. This way I got the best of both worlds in these two very different kinds of riding.

I can tell you one of the other naughty things we got up to as well. In these days swimming in the nude seems to be the thing that everyone does, but when I was a mere eleven years old and I had Silver Fish and David Stanmore had his pony called Twilight, young people only did it where they were sure they wouldn't be caught. Many a summer evening David and I would ride across his father's fields to the secluded banks of the River Test, which was a very popular place for teenagers to go swimming in the buff. While all the big boys – and some girls as well sometimes – were in the river swimming, David and I would swoop down like wolves on the fold and pinch their clothes and hide them in other places. It was a great delight to us to see these bigger youngsters – and particularly the girls – scurrying round the bushes, trying not to be seen, looking for their clothes. We never stole the clothes – we just misplaced them a bit!

# 5 Horses I Cut my Teeth on

I have told you in chapter 4 how I started riding as a seven-year-old on Silver Fish at Lyndhurst down in the New Forest, but now I want to explain things in rather more detail.

When I was ten, rising eleven, Dad decided that I should go show jumping and so he bought me Just Jane. I won the JC championship on her at the Herriard Park Horse Show, near Basingstoke, which used to be run by the late Gerald Barnes and his dear wife. Just Jane was my very first jumping horse and although I loved her there is no doubt that she was a bit of a donkey, but being a kid and riding by the seat of my pants I managed to get half a tune out of her. After that father bought me a very nappy mare called Melody. These were two difficult, if dear, old mares on which to break in any kid, I can tell you. I had to do a lot of whacking, but somehow I got them round. When I proved I could win on them, my father sold the pair of them and bought me a marvellous pony called Nipper from George Hobbs, my riding instructor.

George Hobbs was a tremendous help to me right up to the day he died. Dear George – I put a great deal of what I know today down to George, although he wasn't my first teacher. That was Mr Paterson, as I have mentioned, to whom I went, together with Sue Cohen, who is now Sue Welch, for some years from when I was about nine until I was about eleven or twelve.

George taught me so many more things. Above all he taught me how to school horses and very importantly he taught me a great deal about their make-up – how they move, and all about their backs and hocks and withers and so on. George was a very knowledgeable man, but unfortunately he died when he was only in his early fifties and I am sure that had he been spared a little longer he would have been recognized as one of the best horse physiotherapists we have ever known, and particularly when it came to show jumpers.

I had Nipper from when I was twelve or so to when I was fifteen, which was when I came out of ponies and went on to horses. In the meantime I brought on another pony called Miss Polly Flinders that my father bought off a dealer called Percy Podger from Godalming. She cost £250, which was a pretty good price for a pony in those days, but how much Nipper had cost I have no idea, except that it must have been a lot more than that because my father believed that to be good yourself you had to have something good under you, and Nipper was about the best that money could buy at that time. I think I can say without boasting that I won every major pony class in Southern England on Nipper except perhaps the appropriate event at the Horse of the Year Show, which in those days was held at Harringay in London under floodlights. I only jumped once at Harringay and that was in the last year they were there.

The International Horse Show, which is now the Royal International, was held then at the now defunct White City. It was nostalgia for those old days that recently brought the Royal International back there, but it was not a success. You cannot turn the clock back. I went to the White City on Nipper just once, something which I remember rather well because uncharacteristically I fell off the little beast and so had no chance of winning.

As well as these ponies like Nipper, I rode others such as Blue Mist who was 13.2 hands high and a very genuine pony. I rode him a lot at George Hobbs's place together with Blue Smoke, but I didn't actually have a great number of different mounts when I was in ponies. It was not until I graduated on to horses that the variety of horses I was able to ride increased – it is always good for a rider to have a lot of different horses to ride.

I remember that at fifteen I had a great big donkey of a horse called Pennies from Heaven. He was my very first 'open' horse, which took me into foxhunter classes, and then I had another one called High Spirit plus one or two others that father bought me, but they were never much good as they were such cheap old things. Dad, having paid out so much for Nipper, didn't pay all that much for them – it must have been a lot less than the £250 which was then the going rate for quite a good horse.

I rode these horses for nearly a couple of years, but then I became crazy about farming and wanted to give up show jumping. In the meantime we'd moved to Little Holbury, right in the shadow of the Esso oil refinery at Fawley, at the entrance to Southampton Water. Little Holbury lies on the Roman road that runs up from Lepe, at the entrance to the Beaulieu River, to Southampton, and is right on the eastern edge of the New Forest. From Little Holbury you look across the Solent to where the great lump of the Isle of Wight sprouts out of the sea. But we didn't stay there very long before we were on the move again. This time it was to Wooton Bassett in Wiltshire and of course I took my horses with me, but I have to admit that at that time I was far more interested in farming than I was in horses.

Indeed, as I became more independent, I gave up horses, and that really upset my father. So much so that we were never very close to one another again. Now that I look back on it, I'm not sure we were ever really very great pals. I felt that Dad had pushed me into show jumping because I could win and he liked to bask in the reflected glory.

Being seventeen and just finding my feet, I was out with the girls and into Young Farmers' clubs. In fact I was vice chairman of the Brockenhurst Young Farmers' Club for a year when we lived at Little Holbury, and when we moved to Wooton Bassett, I joined the Calne Young Farmers' Club. I was really at loggerheads with my father at that time and I was sure he was too strict with me because he didn't approve of me being out late on dates with girls as so many of my friends were. Then one day, after a blazing row over some girl or other I had been out with, I decided I'd had enough and I upped and left home.

This meant that I had to earn my own living and do whatever jobs came my way. I worked on a farm for a while and then for a haulage contractor, after which I got a job as a coalman. I worked for British Beef in Swindon, both on their lorries and in the slaughterhouse, and went contract straw-carting with a friend – so many different jobs in order to earn my keep. I even had a spell with the Pressed Steel Company producing car bodies. This was when the Morris 1000 was the most popular car in the country and I had to work with a gang in the pressed steel shop knocking out the car bodies and bonnets.

For this period of my life, from when I was seventeen right through until I was twenty-four, I hardly looked at a horse. I can sort of understand Dad being a bit upset that after all the promise I had shown I had reacted so strongly against him and the horses that he had bought for me, but it was a stage that I think was in some ways necessary as it gave me time to think about what I really ought to be doing with my life. There's a great deal more that I could tell you about this period, but as it has nothing much to do with my career as a show jumper I won't dwell on it.

However there are some aspects of my life at this time which did have considerable bearing on my future career. In my last year of school I spent a lot of time with Mr Parr, the village blacksmith, and earlier than that, when I was twelve, I spent a considerable amount of time with Mr Powell, who was the blacksmith in Totton and who made shoes for the showing trade. As I was only a youngster Mr Powell would never let me knock the shoes on, which was understandable. I was older now and Mr Parr had me nailing shoes on, and so I learned to be a farrier as a kind of unpaid apprentice. It was this experience that had me deciding, when I was twenty-four and fed up with knocking about from one job to another, that slaving for others was not for me. If I was going to work like a slave then it might just as well be for myself, so I decided to make a complete break and start out in business on my own.

I had moved around all over the South of England in pursuit of work, and at this particular time I was living at Shrivenham with a friend of mine called Paul Nichols and his wife Claudie. Paul unfortunately broke up with Claudie, but has since remarried and has a good butchery business in Swindon. It was while I was staying there that one night I got a bit homesick and decided to ring my mother. I wanted to have a chat with her because I was in a terrible state of indecision.

I had half decided to emigrate to Australia, together with two other lads, and become a truck driver. One of them was taken ill, however, and couldn't attempt the trip and then I got cold feet, which was why the prodigal son felt that, despite what had happened in the past, there was no place quite like home. So there was Mum on the end of the phone asking me to come back and live with them, and there was I agreeing.

After I had left home my father had sold the farm at Wooton Bassett and they had moved to Horndean, north of Portsmouth, which, in case you don't know the area, is not all that far east of where I started life at Totton. So it was that Mother and Father came and picked me up and I went back home. Dad was still in the butchery business which he was running with my brother and I decided that when I got back home I would stay for a couple of days to see how things went. I still was half decided to go to Australia, but then my father in confidence dropped the bombshell that my mother had only about six or seven years to live. She had a skin complaint and one or two other things wrong, and the doctors had told my father that she could only be expected to live for a few more years.

Faced with that revelation, how could I go off again so soon? So I stayed. Heaven knows why when I look back on it, because I was like a fish out of water at home. There I was working week after week in the butcher's shop and hating every minute of it. This was not what I was cut out for, and so I compromised. I went out and with my father's help bought myself an Austin A45 pick-up truck and went back to work for Mr Parr at Brockenhurst, which was a good forty miles away from Horndean. So I was living at home but working away.

I suppose I was always being pulled back to the New Forest because it felt so much like home. When you have been brought up in those beautiful surroundings and when your first great outing on a pony was with one of the great hunts of the area – even if it did end in a bit of a disaster – the place tugs at your heart strings. Horndean is a little place whose main claims to fame as far as I was concerned were that it lay on the A3 trunk road so the communications were good and it housed Long's brewery. The hoppy smell from the chimneys of a brewery always makes me think of Horndean. However, Horndean was not home for me. Nor was it a happy place at that time. Dad had the thought hanging over him that Mum could not last very much longer and that then he would be left on his own, so he was in low spirits, and I always felt at a disadvantage because my brother had stayed at home and been a good boy while I had hoofed off and left the family in the lurch.

So it is not surprising that despite the distance which I had to travel I was glad to be working back in the Forest and with Mr Parr whom I knew from days gone by. The road from Horndean to Brockenhurst used to be a bad one for quite a bit of its length because it carried the traffic between the two big ports of Portsmouth and Southampton. Yet once you shook clear of that at, strangely enough, Totton, and you crossed the big bridge that spans the River Test, there was another world. Sudden transformation from town to country. I always felt I was going home when I made that journey.

For Mr Parr I was driving all over the Forest and its surroundings, and of all the times of day perhaps the early mornings were the best. For that is when the mist lay across the open stretches that flanked the totally unfenced roads and made the groups of trees and bushes stand out one behind the other as if they were made of dun-coloured cardboard. You never notice the way they do this, and which lot of trees is behind which other lot, until the silver mist of morning sets them up for you. And then there were the winter mornings when the early sun would sparkle across the grass and the hoar frost would dress up the trees as if it were fairyland.

Lyndhurst may be the Gateway to the Forest, but Brockenhurst is the undeclared capital when it comes to all those truly country pursuits that the Forest has kept fresh and green. It's here that Jennie Loreston Clark, the top dressage rider, has her stables, and it is also the home of the New Forest Hounds. You cannot be part of the Forest, as I was, and not tend towards all those things that have to do with horses. There was no more chance that with my background I could have turned my back on horses completely than that I could have flown off to the moon.

But to get back to the story. Every day for three or more months I banged on shoes for Mr Parr. But I wanted to be my own boss, so in the meantime I borrowed the money off my father and bought a paddock in Catherington Lane, which formed part of the grounds of Merchiston Hall, one of the stately houses in Horndean. It was a big walled-in garden with three stables and a large outbuilding which I turned into a forge and another outbuilding which I converted into two more stables. Thus it was that I left Mr Parr and set up on my own in the business of shoeing horses.

I was very lucky in the line I had adopted because there was very little competition, and a few adverts in the local paper brought me in lots of work. So much so that I found myself snowed under with jobs. My shoeing business absolutely boomed. Amongst other individual jobs I got the contract to shoe the beach ponies on the sands of Hayling Island, plus a similar set of ponies on the beaches of the Isle of Wight, plus the fifty-three horses and ponies that constituted Miss Orbison's riding and trekking centre on the island. So at this time I spent a lot of time by the seaside, although it was hardly a holiday.

On the contrary it was very hard graft. Believe me, I did work hard. All right I was young and in my twenty-fifth year, but I worked like an absolute slave. I may have given up all the odd-jobs I had done previously so as not to be a slave to an employer, but now here I was worse than a slave to my own business. Yet when you work for yourself you can work on knowing that what you are making you are making for yourself and no one else – except the taxman.

I worked seven days a week. Three of those days I spent making shoes and the other four I would be out there banging them on. I established some kind of record, a personal one if not a British or world record, by shoeing no less than twenty-two horses and ponies in one day – all on my own, with no help from anyone. How I did it I don't quite know, because nowadays I couldn't manage to shoe eleven, much less twice that number. In fact, thinking about it I reckon that if I could get through half a dozen I would be doing well. So that particular day I must have been totally inspired.

It was at about this time that my brother left home, having been in effect given the sack by my father, and he was working laying roads for the Council. It was a bit of a funny set-up because, although he had had this bust-up with Dad, he was still living at home with us at Horndean. As for me, things were moving, for it was now that I acquired my much-loved Tuffet and began to do a little show jumping again. I had to ride any horse I could get, but shoeing had to come first because I needed the money, and one thing I needed the money for was to buy a horse box to take Tuffet and any other horses I might have around to the shows.

So it was that I went to a Mr Jack Turner who was a local haulage contractor and he had a little old Bedford in the yard which was all but worked out. I remember that I sat down and argued and cajoled and pleaded with this chap to let me have this lorry at a price that I thought I could afford. Eventually I got him down to £250 and we shook hands on it. Then I said to him 'Well, Mr Turner, I've bought your lorry for £250, but do you mind if I don't pay you for a day or two?' He was a dear little man and he looked at me with mock severity. 'You cheeky little bugger,' he said – and that was strong language because I know for a fact that he very rarely swore. 'You've wasted all my Sunday morning arguing about the price of this lorry and now that we've agreed a price and we've shook hands on it you can't afford to pay for it. Take the damn thing and pay me when you *can* afford it!'

So I got a clapped-out old lorry, which wasn't very much good, but it did allow me to get about to the shows and that began to fire me with enthusiasm again for the show jumping game. I bought another horse called Costa Brava – the same one that I was riding at the time when I first met Pam. He was my own horse, but I got other rides as well. I remember one night going to see a horse owned by a certain Commander Newnham at a place just outside Petersfield. It was a grey horse that he had for sale called His Excellency and I found that I could ride him quite well. He was a very nice ride and a beautiful mount, but he was not as beautiful as the Commander's daughter. Perhaps it was because it was night-time, but I was sure that I had never seen a girl as attractive as this one. She was absolutely gorgeous.

So I rode the horse with my mind not too deeply on my work and then Mrs Newnham decided that she really couldn't part with the animal, but would I ride it for them? As I found both horse and filly so attractive I readily agreed. I rode His Excellency all that season and in the meantime I also worked for a time riding for John Webb, a haulage contractor at Swindon. John's daughter Carol had fallen off and broken her leg and couldn't ride, so John asked me if I would take over her horses until she mended. They had a little grey called Toy Balloon and another very, very naughty horse called Just a Gamble. He was well named, for if you gave him half a chance he would set his jaw and run straight out of the ring with you.

He was just one of the many. Almost every horse I rode at that time was a dodge. Luckily Tuffet was a genuine novice and had no real vices, but he had a lot to learn. Others were not so pleasant. There was for instance one horse of John's called Friendly Too who was not exactly given to living up to his name and had a nasty stop in him. I just couldn't get him going at all and I had to work very hard against all the various problems that these various mounts threw at me. Yet while I cursed and swore at the poor bloody animals, I learned a great deal about handling difficult mounts, which was to stand me in good stead in times to come.

# 6 Back to Show Jumping

After my horseless years of the late fifties I began to come back into the show jumping scene in the early sixties. Not that it had been a completely barren time from an equestrian point of view. I had after all been back in the world of horses for some time. As a farrier you are very deeply immersed in it and you learn a tremendous amount about what is going on in the local area as you travel all round the various riding establishments knocking on shoes. This had eased me back into the world of stables and livery yards. It had got the nostalgic smell of horses back into my nostrils and so it was inevitable that after the hiccup in my riding life I should eventually come back to the fold and the saddle.

When you jump horses you must have somewhere to practise. We didn't have a field, but the local publican John Perkiss had one next door to his pub, and by this time I had made a few rather unprofessional-looking show jumps. I made them out of what I had to hand – bits of timber that happened to be lying around, plus some boxes, together with rough poles and a set of cups to rest them in.

Now there was a problem with John's field in that it was not very big – about three acres in all, I suppose – but it was surrounded by the land of a local farmer called Ted Heath. Ted was very decent to me because the bit of land where I built the stables was originally part of Heath's farm, but a bit for which he had no real use at that time.

Now Ted allowed me to build show jumps, both coloured and rustic, in between Johnny Perkiss's field and his field so that I could give my horses jumping practice over a longer circuit. This proved to be pretty satisfactory because a field soon gets cut up when it rains and you need a good deal of room so that you can vary your courses and not jump over the same areas too much. I used this arrangement during the summer, but in the winter when the fields began to get sticky I transferred operations to Ted's copse behind the church. This copse was covered by tall trees below which little or no grass grew and so it stayed reasonably hard when the grassy fields would have been unusable because of the wet.

Next door to the copse was the bottom of the vicarage garden and I needed more jumping room. Ted made no objections when I asked to build a natural fence in the hedge between his field and the vicarage garden. I suppose it was a bit cheeky not to ask the vicar, but he was no gardener and the bottom of his garden was a long way from the vicarage itself so he never noticed. Or if he did, Christian charity prevented him from saying anything to me about it.

So Ted's copse was a good place to school my horses during the winter months. It was well away from the road and so there was little or no disturbance from passing traffic. In addition Ted's father, whose land it actually was, never actually saw that horses were being jumped on that part of his property. Ted, being only just a little older than me, encouraged me to use the place as my own and made sure that his father never came down to look at what was going on in his copse. Equally the vicar never came to see what was going on at the bottom of his garden as I jumped my horses out of Ted's coppice and into the vicarage garden and back again.

The horses in question were the Newnhams' grey His Excellency and a horse called Commando which I purchased from Jane Pochin, who is now Jan Lanny. These two mounts went quite well for me and I was very happy with them, though I can't say I felt the same about my family. I just didn't seem to have a home life as such, and while my parents did things for me, I always had this desire that they should show me more simple affection than I actually got. As a son, I needed more than just material possessions from them.

Thanks to the intervention of my mother a limited company, Lionel Dunning (Horndean) Ltd, had been formed to sell tack, but while her intentions were good, all it did was to make me feel more enmeshed in the web of home when every instinct I had was telling me to break free and get going on my own.

Not that everything was bad. I had a lucky break because

Commander Newnham not only paid me to ride his horses, but also to perform another, to him, highly important duty. Every other Monday morning I had to report to him what was happening on the boy-friend front as far as his daughter Nicky was concerned. The dear old boy was absolutely petrified that his lovely daughter would up and marry some long-haired layabout and the two of them would run off with all his money. This was I think because he had settled a very large bequest on her when she came of age, which in those days was twenty-one.

So as well as paying me to ride his horses Commander Newnham was also using me as a kind of chaperone for his daughter, which, seeing that she was rich and I was as poor as a church mouse and she was very beautiful into the bargain, might not have been, for him, such a good idea. In actual fact we had a kind of brother-sister relationship which had not the faintest chance of blossoming into romance because there was a vast difference in our social status. For example she had an expensive sports car while I had a clapped-out horse box for transport. Yet, despite all that, we were great friends for the three years that I rode for the Newnhams, and I still see her around the shows.

Now as well as the Newnhams' and other people's horses I had been riding George Hobbs's horses but that was only because George himself had fallen off and broken his leg. Now that his leg was mended I lost those rides. This was a blow as I had enjoyed great success on George's horses. To give you an example, I went to the Royal Isle of Wight Show one year and ended up first, second and third. I won the big event on George's horse Shandrum and came second and third on Tuffet and Costa Brava. Believe me, though, I learned so much from George. He may not have been able to ride the horses himself, but he was always there with me giving advice and encouragement, and so was his brother Wally. Wally was a kind of *chef d'équipe* behind the Hobbs team and the two of them taught me a vast amount about the techniques of training horses which of course over the intervening years has had to be adapted somewhat and modernized to keep abreast of modern-day jumping. Yet that basic grounding from such knowledgeable men has always stood me in good stead. Wally taught me a great deal about training the rider as well as the horse. It is so important to be able to express to the rider what you can see happening and what he or she can do to put it right. Amazingly enough, Wally never rode a horse in his life and yet when it came to training rider and horse he was one of the best of his era.

So that year, thanks to my luck in getting in with the Hobbses, I received a wonderful grounding in the techniques I would need in the future. Sometimes I would have the horses over at George's yard near Hayward's Heath in Sussex, and at others I would have them in my own stables in Horndean. As I was shoeing at the same time I had to be home at least three days a week to keep the farriery business going. So, what with sometimes riding horses in Sussex and sometimes riding them in Hampshire, and shoeing other people's horses at the same time, I was kept very, very busy. It may have been a very tiring life, but I enjoyed it because I was back with horses and making a success of jumping them again.

Soon after George's leg mended he struck up an association with Phil Harris, better known as the name behind the Harris Carpets sponsorship of David Broome. Phil had a large number of horses at that time and a good number of these were at the David Barker establishment. Now I don't know quite what happened, but the Harris horses were taken away from David Barker and went to George Hobbs.

Thus it was that one morning I had a phone call from George asking me if I wanted some horses. I said yes to anything in those days, so long as it had four legs and a head and the ability to jump a bit, so of course it didn't take me long to get over to George's yard and pick up no less than four of Phil Harris's horses on what I hoped was a semi-permanent loan. I cannot quite remember what all their names were now, but certainly one was called Bonsoir. With the horses came all their tack, rugs and so on, yet even better than that was a brand new Austin lorry. That was an absolute gift from the gods. My old lorry had never been very marvellous in the first place, and it was now getting mighty rough, so to have a brand new lorry to drive was, for me, absolute luxury.

Thus in yet another way George was good to me, and I rode

Phil Harris's horses for all that season. However Phil had let George have the horses on the understanding that he (George) would sell them for him and by the end of that season they had all been sold on, as had my luxury lorry which was also only on loan.

Amongst the Harris horses that were sold was one called Battling Pedulus who, if he had remained sound, would have been one of the all-time greats. He was, to my mind, an absolutely fabulous horse, quite fantastic, but unfortunately he got pedal ostitis early in life and so he had only a short career as a show jumper. Battling Pedulus was perhaps the first really top horse that Phil Harris ever owned, but now of course he owns, or has owned, some of the best horses in Europe.

Bonsoir, whom I mentioned earlier, was sold to Italy and became a top-flight jumper. It jumped on the Italian international team, but when I went to Rome with the British squad in 1973 I had the unhappy experience of seeing the horse which I had once ridden involved in an accident so serious that the poor animal had to be put down.

The sale of the Harris horses was followed by Nicky Newnham's decision to give up show jumping. This was truly bad news for me because not only did I lose most of my good rides, but also the livery money for them, which was bringing me in quite a good living. However you cannot keep a Dunning down for long, and I bought a horse called November Morning at the Epsom Horse Show. She was a dark brown mare and rather scatty, and I must have thought she was worth having because I paid the vast sum of £1,200 for her, which was all the realizable money I had in the world at that time. I bought her from a girl called Susan Kane, who was Willy Carson's girl friend for some years.

I schooled that mare for four or five weeks and then I took her to the Kent County Show and she went fantastically. I remember I won the Burnham Bowl on her. I won the Have a Gamble competition (which today is called a Top Score competition), and I also won a speed class, so that my total winnings came to no less than £1,250. She was the first horse I ever owned that won me as much money as she cost – and that at the first big show I took her to!

However it isn't just success stories like this that stand out in my mind. In the early winter of 1969 I experienced a catastrophic loss. I needed somewhere to winter my horses and, not for the first time, my friend Mr Hartley, the vet, helped by allowing me to put four of them in one of his fields. It was quite a good field and had a solid shed for shelter. As it was immediately next to Mr Hartley's house, he was going to be able to keep an eye on them for me. I remember being strangely uneasy in my mind as I drove Tuffet, Hedgehopper, Costa Brava and Polly XX up to the field in my horse box. There was no reason at all why I should have had any qualms about doing this because, as I say, everything seemed as right as rain with the quarters I was taking them to. Even so I did not feel at all happy about things. Yet, as you do, I turned the horses out and left them because I told myself that these silly hunches were just that – silly hunches.

They hadn't been out there for much more than a week before I had this phone call from Mr Hartley. He told me that his man had been out to feed my horses and that Polly had kicked Costa Brava. 'Oh dear,' I said. 'Is he badly hurt?' Hesitantly Mr Hartley replied, 'Well it's a little bit worse than that. You see she kicked him very hard and when their legs connected she broke her hind leg and he broke his front fetlock joint.'

When such things happen to horses there is nothing to be done but have them put down, which Mr Hartley, being a vet, had to do. There's an old saying in the horse world 'no foot – no horse', and it is very, very true indeed because nothing is so certain to end the life of a show jumping horse than that it gets into trouble with its legs. It was a tragic blow to me and also a great financial loss because neither of them was insured and so I lost a lot of money as well as half of my string.

It is always upsetting to lose a horse, but the death of Polly was a poignant one for me as she was a little chestnut mare who was a bit hot (in the way I like), and she was the horse on which I won my first few big classes. Your first major successes are never forgotten, and you treasure the memory of the horses that brought them to you, and so I felt Polly's loss particularly deeply. I had won classes on her at the Bournemouth Show, at

Woburn Abbey, at Hillingdon and many others. Her big problem was that she was difficult to get round the first time because she had a little bit of a stop in her, but she was very, very careful and if I could get her round the first time then the winning of the jump-off and of later classes was always quite easy for her.

Incidentally, it was when I took Polly to the Woburn Abbey Horse Show that I first met Harvey Smith in any way to get to know him. Harvey had, in characteristic manner, just swapped a horse for a dog. It was a lurcher, and after the jumping on the first night I went with Harvey 'lamping' after rabbits around the Duke of Bedford's estate with this newly acquired lurcher. The car we went in had been borrowed by Harvey on the pretext that he wanted to try it for a couple of days, but all he really wanted it for was to go rabbiting around the grounds of Woburn Abbey.

You will recall that I mentioned a horse called Commando whom I bought from Jane Lanny. I sold him on to go to Italy and he won the Grand Prix in Rome. That was another famous first – the first horse I ever owned and rode who went on into the big time. It was a thing that made me wish I had never sold the horse in the first place, but it also gave me the idea that maybe I too had the ability to school on horses and give them the basics of what it takes to go right to the top. I had the feeling even more strongly when another horse which I sold on to Italy did well in the 1980 Olympics.

So as the swinging sixties ended and the seventies dawned I was back into show jumping and making a success of it, as well as building a confident hope that maybe Lionel Dunning could get his name writ large in the upper echelons of the show jumping world. I had had my tragedies, but it was a great time for looking forward and for realizing that I too had the ability, like George Hobbs, not only to ride horses but also to produce them to a standard that was international.

# 7 Where my Caravan has Rested

I shall never forget the first time I bought a caravan. I went to various establishments to look for caravans and in the end I bought a very old Berkley. It was very strong and very clean, but quite old and it cost all of £25, which in those days was a lot of money for an old caravan. It was strong enough to do the job and I had a drawbar welded on to the back of my lorry.

By this time I had sold my Bedford and had bought a Commer from Michael Cresswell. I had gained a good deal of experience of Commers because when I was driving for Webbs and others it was always Commers that I had been using. They had an aluminium two-stroke engine which made a real roaring noise and the one I had also had an aluminium body. It wasn't exactly a pretty thing, but it got me around and did the job I asked of it for several years.

The first time I used the caravan behind the lorry I decided I would do a tour of the West Country shows and so off I set with some four horses up and the caravan behind. Every thirty miles or so I would stop and take a look at the caravan to see that it was taking the strain.

Now that I had a caravan and could extend my range of action I was sure I had arrived. I had visions of myself as a top-name show jumper ranking beside great names like Harvey Smith and David Broome. There was only one great difference: they had already arrived and I was starting at the bottom and trying to work up.

However I did pretty well on that tour, winning many classes at shows at Gillingham, Shaftesbury, Bournemouth and Mel-plash, which is a village near Beaminster in Dorset, and I felt quite pleased with myself! Also none of the problems which I feared might arise with a caravan materialized, so all in all it was a successful tour.

At that time my groom was a girl called Carol Quatermain,

and poor Carol only got paid her wages when we won. I paid her £5 a week and sometimes, when I was short of money, she wouldn't get paid for several weeks on end. However she didn't let me forget. If we went to a show and won, I would arrive sometimes at the secretary's tent to claim my winnings only to find that Carol had got there first so she could take her wages out of the money before I got my sticky fingers on it. She was a very good girl, though, and she stayed with me for about three years.

The very first time I went to Hickstead I went in my Bedford lorry with my Berkley caravan on the back. I was going through Cowdray Park on a very narrow road and bang – a tyre blew. There I was stuck on this narrow road with four horses on the lorry and a caravan with a blown tyre – and no spare wheel! Well I don't need to tell you that I really was getting in a state. Along came the police and they began to officiate with flashing beacons and a one-way system, plus a live policeman directing traffic. But what was I to do?

Luckily, just then along came the British Army and, because my caravan was one of the originals that had big wheels, they had a spare that fitted it. The officer-in-charge was luckily a sergeant who was into the ways of the Army and he assured me that he would be able 'to lose a wheel here and there'. So gratefully I slipped him a fiver and went on my way to Hickstead where I remember I had a pretty good show.

After the show I backed my lorry up to my caravan, hitched up and drove off. I don't know why I should have noticed it at that point, but as I drove out of Hickstead gate, to my horror I could see that there was no caravan. Luckily when the tow-bar snapped I had only been travelling slowly and the van had not done any damage to itself or anyone else, but it was a frightening experience I can tell you.

The reason the tow-bar snapped was that it was a rigid one and the whip between it and the caravan had caused it to shear. Nowadays we always have a spring-loaded draw-bar and that was what I converted the lorry to after this incident. I left the caravan at Hickstead and got a friend to go down in his Land-Rover to bring it back for me.

Once I went to Shepton Mallet Horse Show and coming out

of Shepton Mallet all the lights on the lorry went out. I was still living at Horndean on the other side of Hampshire then and that is quite a way from Somerset across Wiltshire and most of Hampshire. However I had left the show early and although I really needed sidelights I could get by without any lights so long as I didn't get caught. It was midsummer and so it stayed light till quite late and we got all the way to Winchester and beyond before anything went wrong. Now the road from Winchester to Horndean is a back road and so I soldiered on with no lights, but as luck would have it the old lorry broke down along the way. It came to a halt on a blind bend and all I could do was to hang a torch on the back-end of the caravan and hope.

Now I had happened to break down just by some gallops that belonged to Bill Wightman and as I struggled to make the stubborn old lorry go I heard a car coming at tremendous speed down the road. It roared round the corner and I could see it was a souped-up Mini. The driver managed to see the caravan in time, but he swerved into the off-side verge where he leaped the ditch, went through the hedge and on to the gallops. You would have expected him to stop, but not a bit of it. Off down the gallops he sped and I never did know what happened to him. I think now that he must have had a bit of drink inside him, so he didn't dare stop to see what damage he'd done, which luckily was not much. Anyway I managed to get going and arrived home without hitting anything or anything hitting me. I didn't meet any policemen either, which was very lucky for me, though your luck has to run out sometimes.

I thought it had the time Pam and I were coming home from Harwood Hall one night in another Bedford lorry. We were steaming up the A1 when I began to get problems with my lights. Soon the lights failed completely, but I managed to stick in the slow lane between a couple of big lorries who contributed my headlights and tail lights. However eventually I had to turn off to Marston which is the next village to Brant Broughton and so we were now on our own without a light. We got as far as the crossroads to our village and sure enough along comes the 'Old Bill'. He pulls up and stops me. 'And where do you think you're going?'

'I'm going home,' I said.

'Where have you come from?'

'Harwood Hall.'

'How long have you had no lights?'

'For the last ten miles.' Now this was a bit of a lie because it was more like thirty miles, but I suppose he felt I hadn't tried to flannel my way out of it.

'Well for god's sake get off the road,' he said, 'because if not I'll have to book you.'

With that he jumped in his car and sped off to find some other law-breaker while I drove up the road to home thanking my lucky stars for the good sense of English coppers.

When I got picked to go to the Berlin Show in 1970 with the British team my father wanted to come with me. He didn't fancy staying in hotels and so he suggested we take the caravan. Which was all very well, but it was a helluva long way to Berlin with a small horse box and a caravan behind. Maximum speed for this set-up was about fifty miles an hour and it was going to take a long, long time.

So off we went to Berlin. In those days I had The Bijou, who was a very good speed horse and one that could also get a fair bit of height in puissance events. I had His Excellency and Tuffet, and they stood up to the journey quite well. We travelled across Europe and eventually arrived at the East German border. My father was a bit nervous, but he had to get out to spend a penny where we had stopped under the watchful eyes of gun-toting border guards. While he was in the loo the officious guards made us move the lorry to the other side of the lavatory block from the one where we had stopped.

I shall never forget the look of horror on my dad's face when he came out of that loo and thought we'd gone off without him. When he realized that we'd only moved round the other side he didn't waste a moment, but made a bee-line for the lorry, jumped in and never stirred from the cab again.

So Dad held his water and stayed in the cab all the way to Berlin, and as we travelled the weather went really cold. Overnight it was about twenty-two degrees of frost and by the time we arrived the draw-bar was frozen so that we couldn't unhitch the caravan. However, we were able to unload the horses and get them into their stables and I went back to see my father at the caravan. He was struggling to get the jacks down, but they were also frozen up. Eventually we did get them down and could get into the van.

When we opened the door what a sight met our eyes. It was a complete shambles inside, for everything that moved had been shaken out of its place and into a heap on the floor. Not only had the eggs frozen and split, but the tins of fruit etc. had also frozen and split open and spilt their contents on to the floor. Even the gas had frozen. It was really a complete disaster and there was no way in which we could sleep in that caravan.

When I went and told my story to the secretary of the show, I was told that a room had been reserved for us in the hotel. However, my father had completely set his face against paying for hotel accommodation and so he ended up bedding down with the grooms rather than pay up. This put me in a spot because I couldn't think of myself enjoying the comfort and warmth of the hotel when my father was down there under the arena. So I ended up down there as well, with no one to talk to other than my father and no contact with the other riders. To make matters worse, everyone down in the grooms' quarters spoke German and neither of us could make out a word of what was being said.

The first sight of the massive course in the Deutschlandhalle really put the wind up me. It was indoors and early in the season, and I knew that my two horses, His Excellency and Tuffet, were not really prepared for courses of twelve or more massive fences, some of which had six-foot spreads. But that was what Micky Brinkmann built and that was what we were there to contend with. Unlike most course-builders today, Brinkman used to employ a couple of his fences twice in a round so as to get the length, although the arena of the Deutschland-halle seemed vast compared to, say, the Wembley arena. The place seated 16,000 spectators and the jumping arena was some 77 yards by 50 yards, compared to Wembley's 70 yards by 28 yards with seating for only 9,000 people.

Anyway it was February and the icy winds did not help much to lift my spirits. Anneli Drummond-Hay completed our trio with Harvey, but she was up against a heavy cold which could well have been flu. Her famous horse Merely-a-Monarch jumped out of his skin to give them a place in every class they entered, and Anneli was top on points for the Grand Prix and had a marvellous position in the starting order, being fourth from last. However disaster struck in the shape of the pills she took to combat the bug she had picked up. It completely destroyed her judgement so that she crashed out after the third fence – a terrible disappointment. However she made up for it in the Golden Bracelet, which was for girls only, when she beat Janou Lefebvre into second place, while she herself also got third place on her other six-year-old mare Fanella Freya.

Of course I cannot forget how Harvey's horse box broke down at Helmstedt which meant that his horses, O'Malley and Ripcord, arrived long after he did and he had to sit there and watch on the first night because the horses were still somewhere on the road. Even so Harvey didn't have too bad a show, being placed in all the Grand Prix qualifiers and winning one of them. O'Malley was a good puissance horse and came third in the puissance event which was no disgrace in so far as the wall went up to seven feet in the end. Harvey had one rather spectacular fall when O'Malley tipped him into one of Brinkman's big parallels, but both horse and rider were tough characters and neither suffered any real damage. Incidentally, Graziano Mancinelli won the puissance on his big bay Water Surfer splitting with Herman Schridde on Heureka, so Harvey was in effect second.

When I tell you that the Grand Prix was won by the late lamented Hartwig Steenken on that fantastic horse Simona, while Alwin Schockemöhle was second on his equally out-standing animal Donald Rex, you can see what the competition was like. They were on their home ground, and I had driven day and night across Europe to get there. It wasn't the best recipe for total success. Still, by the end of the week I was enjoying myself, putting it all down to experience and giving a good account of myself. The competition was so stiff that even with the fastest time just one pole down knocked me to eighth place in one event. All in all, while I never actually won a class, I was quite pleased to get several thirds and fourths.

I learned a lot from that Berlin trip. I realized that if you are to give of your best then you just cannot knock yourself out trailing across Europe towing a caravan that in the end proved to be more of a liability than an asset. I should have let my father do what he wanted and I should have got real nights' sleep in the hotel so that I was fresh for the trials to come. I also saw that while His Excellency and Tuffet were fine horses, I was, in the future, going to have to get myself better horses, if possible German-bred ones, although an eventual tie-up with Alwin's brother Paul did not materialize for many years. However good you are, in the end you are only as perfect as your horse will let you be. Hartwig and the Schockemöhles had a vast string of great mounts to choose from – at that time I had almost to take what I was given.

Then the show was over and we were off on our way back again through the corridor that connected Berlin with West Germany. It was an awful road with many pot-holes in it and it was a very slow journey. I was following Harvey's lorry, and when we got to Helmstedt we found that Willy Halliway had lost the papers. However we weren't going to let that stop us and we managed to drum up some papers with which we duped the guards because they were half asleep, it being about half-past-three in the morning. The Berlin Show finished about nine at night and you then tried to get through the border posts during the night because the traffic was quiet at that time. By day it was terrible, this being the only land life-line for West Berlin, and Helmstedt itself was a really horrible place to be. It has got better since then, and the border guards are not as officious as they used to be, but in those days all they did was look at you with a gun barrel as they perused your papers – it was quite a frightening experience.

Everything went reasonably well as we crossed Belgium *en route* for Antwerp where we were going to embark. We got about ten miles from Antwerp and then all of a sudden we heard a thud. I looked out to see a wheel go bowling past the lorry – my wheel, my caravan wheel, on its way who knew where. We were on a motorway and all I could do was pull in on to the central reservation to survey the damage. It was worse than I thought. No only had I lost the wheel, but the stub axle had sheared and come away with it.

Can you imagine spending the night in a caravan that had lost a wheel in sub-zero temperatures in the middle of the main autoroute from Zeebrugge to Antwerp? Of course we hadn't been there for much more than half an hour when along came the police and we feared the worst, but when they saw our predicament they were quite decent about it and told us that we could stay there until morning, which, seeing that we couldn't move anyway, was a fairly obvious thing to say. They said they would contact a garage, and next morning along came a garage mechanic and jacked the caravan up. Actually he was a very clever fellow because he removed a large chunk of the chassis of the caravan, took it back to his garage, welded it back together again and then refitted it so that it was as good or better than before. It was tremendous luck to be sent such a skilled mechanic. So instead of catching the morning boat we got the afternoon boat and returned to England late, but not much the worse for wear. However I can promise you that that was the first and last time I have ever taken a caravan on the Continent. The roads abroad are populated with maniacs, and on top of that they are not as well maintained as over here and the caravans get shaken to bits.

Despite that I kept that Sprite going right through until I met Pam and for a while afterwards, but then we managed to acquire her mother's Besicar, which was just as well because when we made the lightning move from Jim Byford's farm at Petersfield up to Lincolnshire we needed all the 'removal vans' we could get and having the two caravans helped that operation no end.

When we eventually got settled down in Lincolnshire we sold the Sprite, because Pam was not going to live in a second-rate clapped-out van that had seen its best days. The Besicar was another matter, as it was a lovely caravan, but it had never done much moving about. It had stood out for a long time and unbeknown to us the rain had got into it and it was rotten in places. So much so that returning home from a show at Harwood Hall near Upminster in Essex we were trailing up the A13 towards London when we became aware of a car behind us flashing its lights urgently. So we stopped and I got out to have a look and, unbelievably, the poor old Besicar had split in two and was in such a bad way that we had to abandon it by the side of the road. Eventually I somehow managed to get the old wreck home and, having shored it up underneath and patched it up, I put it outside the house on its jacks with a 'For Sale' notice on it. Then I went to see the bank manager and got a loan to buy myself a new Avondale caravan. Meanwhile the Besicar sat outside the house for several weeks until one day along came a set of travelling people. 'How much for the caravan, Guv?' By this time I was fed up to the back teeth with seeing the thing there and so was everyone else, so I said, 'How about £250?' He was delighted with that. He paid me from a roll of fivers and tenners which he drew out of his greasy back pocket, hitched the caravan to his little truck and was off. I never saw him again, but I half expected to because that van was not the best of buys.

Today we use nothing less than one of the most rugged and at the same time comfortable caravans on the road. It is a four-wheeler, made in Germany, called a Tabbart. There is nothing to touch a four-wheel caravan for the kind of hard trailing we do to shows all over the country, and now, with my wife to manage the domestic side of all this, we travel well and in great comfort. Very different from my first lone foray down into the wilds of the West Country so many years ago.

# 8 I Meet Pam

If anyone had told me how my life would change when I eventually met a girl I really could care about, I would never have believed them. In 1968 I was still at home at Horndean with my father and my brother, running my blacksmith's shop and the saddlery business.

In those days I had Strathdon and Tuffet – dear old Tuffet who is now twenty-four years old and still going strong. Tuffet was not mine but belonged to the late Mr Hartley, the veterinary surgeon. Strathdon on the other hand belonged to the late George Forbes and I had another of his horses called Hedgehopper. As well as these I had an eight-year-old called Costa Brava which I bought from the Royal Marines for £150 and Mr Hartley denerved him because he had navicular disease in both front feet. This is called neurectomy, and if I had wanted to sell Costa Brava on I would have been forced to disclose that this severing of certain sensory nerves within the foot had been done. It is frowned on by some, but providing you keep a very careful eye on the desensitized feet to see that no injury (that the horse cannot feel) has been caused, it is a good way of giving a horse, otherwise destined for the knacker's yard, a new lease of life. Lots of horses have been saved this way and have been ridden hard over fences and across country for years without pain or lameness.

Costa Brava had never done any show jumping when I got him. He was purely what the Marines call a 'charger', but he won a good number of classes for me before he had to be put down after the kicking match with Polly described in chapter 6.

In those days I would ride anybody's horses. Anything that was put in my way I would ride, irrespective of whether it was good, bad or indifferent. I can remember once going to the Aldershot Horse Show, which used to be held on the old show ground at Aldershot off the main road between Aldershot and

Farnham, and there having a really successful show.

On the first day I was jumping Costa Brava, who was then a Grade C horse, not having won enough money to be upgraded to B and certainly nowhere near becoming a Grade A horse. Anyway there were three classes running at the same time in three separate rings. So I first jumped in the class which was for Grade C horses and got a clear round. Then I dashed over to another ring and jumped him in the Scurry and I won that speed class on him.

I also had a horse who was Grade B, but I did not have him at the show, even though I had entered him. Now I suddenly realized that, with the winnings from the classes I had just been in, Costa Brava was now a Grade B horse and so I entered him also for the Grade B competition. Lo and behold, he won that as well. However, as he had jumped clear in the preliminary Grade C class, he was also eligible to go and take part in the proper Grade C event, so I put him in for it. Believe it or not, he won again and so I won all three classes on that one horse on that one day.

Naturally I was ecstatic about this success, and the sun certainly shone on Lionel Dunning that day because Hedge-hopper had also gone well and Tuffet had won the five-bar jumping. Not that everything had gone right. I had a nappy horse called Le Bijou and I managed to get eliminated on him.

The second day was not quite as good as the first, but I can remember being pretty pleased with the way things were going. Then on the third day of the show, while walking the course, I saw a young lady who attracted my eye immediately. She was absolutely immaculately dressed and suddenly I found that my heart was all of a flutter and I remember thinking to myself, 'What a lovely girl!'

As far as I was concerned the girl was not going to get away, and when I saw her go into Mike Saywell's caravan I decided to throw caution to the winds and make myself known. I suppose I gatecrashed a bit, and maybe it wasn't too surprising that she cut me dead. She could hardly bring herself to speak to me. She had gone in to have a chat with Mike, with whom she was friendly, both of them coming as they did from Lincolnshire, and here was this upstart stranger trying to chat her up.

That did not help my confidence very much, I can tell you, but I did not intend to give up. That afternoon I was walking the course for the Area International Trial (AIT), and the new object of my attentions was doing the same. I had found out already that she was called Pamela Coldron, but when once more I tried to make some advances she cut me dead again. Yet I knew even then that this was no ordinary boy meets girl affair, because I remember saying to Alan Oliver, 'You know, Alan, that girl over there is the one I am going to marry one day.' Alan turned and looked me hard between the eyes and he laughed: 'I tell you kid,' he said. 'You couldn't afford to clean her boots.' To which my reply was, 'OK, you wait and see.'

I didn't let my rebuffs by Miss Coldron affect my riding and managed to finish second in the AIT on Strathdon. Pam was riding a very good little horse called November Song, of whom we will hear more later.

Then the show was over, but the memory lingered on. I just couldn't forget her and she was always there at the back of my mind haunting my waking moments and invading my dreams. Yet it all seemed a bit hopeless. She lived two hundred miles away in Lincolnshire. She jumped a different circuit of shows to me. Her mother had just brought her down for the show at Aldershot as a one-off occurrence. There was probably little chance that I would ever see her again.

The 1968 season passed and the 1969 season dawned. I had other girl friends, including Cindy Mead with whom I went out for quite a long time. Even my choice of girl friends was fired by my ambition, because I tried to pick girls who were near the top of the show jumping tree. I figured I could learn more from those who were at the top than from people nearer the bottom. It may not have been a very romantic way of going on, but it indicates how dedicated I was to succeeding in the show jumping world.

Now I look back on it, I was really rather a mercenary guy because I only used to date girls who I thought might be able to help me improve and better myself both in horse knowledge and social status. I had been brought up in a normal middle-class household, but I hankered after being that one bit better. I wanted to be able to mix with high-class people who were not only pleasant to know, but were also much better heeled than myself, and I hoped thereby one day to become one of them.

In the 1969 season I had some good mounts – horses like Smoke Drift, who won me quite a few classes. My string then was not as good as the horses I have today, but I managed pretty well because of my ability to ride difficult horses into top places in the competitions. I had my horse His Excellency, whom I had managed to buy for £800, and he was really good to me, as was the evergreen Tuffet. Tuffet was my backbone – my very best horse. I had him from when I started in foxhunter classes in 1965 right through until I retired him in 1975.

The Timken Horse Show is held at Northampton, which is not too far from Lincoln where Pam lived at home with her parents. So when I went to the Timken that summer I knew I had a real chance of seeing her again, and sure enough there was this same beautiful young lady exercising her horse. After completing her schooling I found her talking to a couple of my own friends and so I was able to mingle and join in the conversation.

I spent all that day trying to break the ice a little with Pam and I suppose it was because I was persistent that I began to get a bit of response. I promise you I was working really hard on this because I was not exactly used to talking to well-educated young ladies. By that I mean people who had had a much better education than I – and in her case a 200 per cent better education.

Luckily that night, after the show was over, Mrs Bradley (Caroline Bradley's mother) was holding a party and I was invited along with the others. David Broome was also going to the party and in those days he was courting Judy Boulter, who is now Judy Pyrah, while Tom Hudson was also there with his wife, and we decided we would all go together.

Tom Hudson is the radio commentator who has always been a pal of mine, and he had his car and offered to take us all to the party. David put me on the spot when he asked, in all innocence, 'Who are you taking to the party Lionel?' to which I replied, 'I don't know but never mind, I'll be taking someone, don't you worry.' That someone I had already decided on, but I had to use some strategy so I went and knocked on the door of

Mrs Coldron's caravan. It was a ploy I had read about in a book on how to handle situations when the lady is proving difficult!

I had to summon a certain amount of courage to confront Pam's mother in her den. I didn't get too wonderful a reception, either. 'Well, what do you want?' was the icy greeting. 'Excuse me Mrs Coldron,' I said hesitantly 'but there's a party for the riders on tonight and I wondered if it would be possible for you to allow me permission to ask your daughter to come with me.'

I could see that they were an old-fashioned, tight-knit family and that if anything was to succeed this almost Victorian approach would do it. I was right, and she warmed considerably, 'Yes my boy, certainly you can take me daughter if you wish, but make sure you are not too late. I want her home early, because we have to be off early in the morning as I have a coffee morning and I do not intend to be late home for that.' So, feeling very cock-a-hoop, I said, 'Thank you very much', and proceeded back to the ring where Pam was riding her horse.

You will realize what it meant to me when I say that never before in the whole wide world had I ever deliberately ducked a class. But this time I took my horse Smoke Drift into the ring with the intention of kicking out a couple of fences so that I would not have to go into the jump-off. That way I figured I could get back quickly into the collecting ring and so have plenty of time to intercept Pam before she perhaps beetled off and so prevented me asking her to go to the party with me. That was the first and only time I have ever done less than my best to win a class, and it just goes to show that I knew deep down that this was make-or-break for my future happiness.

So when I could see she was on her own, and without more ado, I went straight up to her and said, 'Excuse me, but there's a party on tonight and I wonder if you would like to come to it with me?' Just as I had hoped, my strategy worked because Pam looked at me and said, 'No, no I'm afraid I can't. I'd love to, of course, but Mummy would not let me as we have to leave for home early in the morning.' So, to her surprise and horror, I said, 'You needn't worry, Pam, because I've been to see your mother and she says that you are welcome to come with me providing we are not late home and don't make a lot of noise.'

So poor Pam was in a cleft stick. Having said she'd love to come, and as I'd been to see her mother already, she must have realized that she had been outmanoeuvred and with the best of grace replied, 'Thank you then, I'd very much like to come.'

The party went well and we had a lot of fun and I began to feel that I was perhaps getting somewhere at last. This feeling was not too far wrong either, because after we had left the party early, both the other couples also wanting to get relatively early nights, I got dropped off in the dark with Pam and I was rewarded for my evening with a good-night kiss which boosted my morale no end.

Then it was time to part. 'Thank you for a lovely evening,' she said as she turned to walk to her caravan. 'Hope to see you again one day.' Oh dear, those words sounded so final, and it was with an intense feeling of disappointment that I trudged slowly back to my own lonely lorry and wondered if this was the beginning and the end of my romance.

The party had been on the last evening of the British Timken Show and so I was on my way early next morning to another show. But before I went I could not help wandering over to where the Coldrons' caravan had stood. Of course it had been packed, the horse box loaded, and both had long since disappeared back to Lincolnshire so that Pam's mother could run her coffee morning. I was really fed up and lonesome – I could perhaps have got much further than I had if only I could have seen Pam for longer. What in hell's name did her mother have to go and have a coffee morning for when there was a lovelorn swain hanging on her daughter's every word and action? I had taken Pam out once – how would things shape from here? How *could* things shape? I really hadn't the faintest of faint ideas, but I was determined to work on the problem.

As it was fate again took a hand in my romantic affairs by ensuring that when I went to the Millfields Horse Show, to which I had never been before, who should be chatting to one another by the entrance as I went in to walk the course but Pam's father and mine? What chance could have brought my father and what I hoped might be my future father-in-law into conversation I just didn't know, but there they were. So Pam was here too somewhere! Better than that, there I saw her out in the arena walking the course and when I went up to speak to her what a difference in her manner to me. She was now quite charming – totally different from the first rough, tough beginnings. She didn't gush – Pam is not the sort of girl to gush to anyone – but I felt a great stride forward had been made in our relationship. Of course you cannot say much in the time when you are out walking a course, but I was determined that this time I was going to get some more time with her.

After the event, in which incidentally I managed to come second on Smoke Drift to Derek Kent, David Broome said, 'Let's go and have a cup of tea.' So off we all trooped to the restaurant. I made sure that I invited Pam to come as well, but was almost surprised when she agreed – and without any hesitation. So there we all were, sipping tea and talking about our Wembley prospects and also about the Wembley Ball, when David put his big foot in it. In all innocence, because he wasn't aware that my affections had shifted somewhat, David said to me, 'I suppose you are bringing Cindy to the Ball.' If looks could kill, then that would have been the end of David Broome's career, and he soon cottoned on to the fact that the one I wanted to take to the Ball was here with us at the table and he changed his tune a bit.

However, I was still so unsure of what Pam felt for me that I was convinced that irrevocable damage had been done to my shaky romance, and after the show I had to say goodbye to Pam without things having got very much further forward. In fact I was quite convinced that David had, without realizing it, ruined my chances.

This time, however, I was not going to let the grass grow under my feet and I got straight on to the BSJA to find out Pam's number so that I could ring her up. She had never volunteered her phone number and I had never had the nerve to ask for it. It is amazing what love does to you. I can ride horses over the most demanding of courses, risking life and limb in the process, and yet when it came to asking the girl I wanted most in the world for her phone number I just didn't have the courage.

With my heart in my boots I dialled the fatal number and when she came on the phone I hesitantly asked her if she would go to the Horse and Hound Ball at Wembley with me. Joy of joys, she agreed to go! I was so flushed with success I went one stage further and asked her what she was doing the Sunday night before the show. It is customary for the riders to arrive the day before the show starts and so there was a spare evening just begging to be filled. Again she said she wasn't doing very much and would like to come out with me.

Now while others might have got to Wembley during the normal, reasonable daylight hours of Sunday, it had always been my bachelor habit to get there in the middle of Sunday night. Not this year, though. I was there not in time for tea, not in the middle of Sunday afternoon, but by midday, to find the Coldrons' caravan already pulled in.

It didn't take me long to get unloaded and the horses stabled so that I could hurry over to Pam's parents' caravan and make my number.

When I got there I found she was out somewhere talking to some of her friends, so I invited myself into the caravan in order to get my feet under the table so to speak with Mr and Mrs Coldron. I knew that as they were the kind of parents who kept a careful eye on their daughter's welfare, I was not going to get very far unless I could make friends with them. To my surprise I got on absolutely fantastically with both of them and I found that despite a somewhat hard and strict exterior Mrs Coldron was a very nice and understanding woman.

So that night Pam and I were to be found at the pictures seeing *The Valley of the Dolls*. I don't know quite how it happened, but we suddenly both found we needed one another and by the end of that evening I knew that we were both taking it for granted that we would be married. It was truly a whirlwind courtship once it started. We had only spoken to one another a few times before, but here we were in love – not quite at first sight, but certainly now, after the very slow and hesitant start, at a rare old gallop. I was truly amazed at the shine that Pam had taken to me, as I have never thought of myself as a great catch or much of a ladies' man, and I tended to feel that perhaps either she or her parents would think that I was not good enough for the family. Yet now both parents and daughter had capitulated and it was absolutely enchanting.

We went out every night throughout the show, and before it was all over Pam had invited me to a wedding – not ours – but to that of a friend of hers. Of course I jumped at the idea of going, so as to be with her. The only cloud on my sunny horizon just then was my father, who thought I was crazy to court a girl who lived 200 miles from home, but I soon made the arrangements for that weekend by staying at Pam's on the Friday night, going to the wedding on the Saturday and then driving back home on the Sunday.

It was while I was driving back home from that wedding weekend that I realized that I had to make some drastic changes in my life. Despite my age I knew that my silly old father was not going to take kindly to my having a regular girl friend, much less one who would soon be my fiancée. After all it was a girl who had sparked the rift when I was seventeen, and the memory of that was still strong in my mind.

I was in love with Pam, but it did not blind me to the fact that she was a forceful girl who had sharpened her determination over many a cross-country fence as she strove for the top honours in point-to-pointing in the Midlands. Her hot temper and her dogged determination were not going to accord in any way with my home life. For one thing I was sure that my father would be very jealous of Pam's presence if she came to live at or near home when we were married, and I could see really rough times ahead.

Still there was time to make adjustments and I told myself that time would tell, and in the meantime I would look around at the possible alternatives to what I was doing now. Alternatives that would get me away from home so that when it came to it Pam and I would be able to live together in our own place and out of the clutches of home and father. I couldn't quite throw over all at once the business of Lionel Dunning (Horndean) Ltd, which I had been building up for the last six years. We were now at the end of 1970, and what little money I had was invested in the company. We had also between us built a nice house that we could all share and so I was very deeply committed to the family and its business. It would not be easy to get out – yet get out I knew I must.

During that winter I met a chap called Jim Byford who

bought some horses from me as well as a lot of harness. Now he was a stockbroker with Lloyd's of London and he had the money to start farming, but not the know-how. I had always had this thing about farming ever since I was a teenager and I had acquired a fair amount of knowledge of how to run a farm. As Jim Byford was very interested in show jumping, it seemed a very good idea when he suggested that we buy a farm. I could bring my horses there, run the farm for him and at the same time go on with my show jumping.

We started to look for a farm in the spring of 1971. Naturally my father was very much against this, and as time went on I found myself once again shut out from the family. The following Christmas Day I stayed at home with my father and brother, but on Boxing Day I drove up to Pam's place and spent the next few days with her. The contrast of the joy and happiness that I found with Pam to the claustrophobic conditions at home only heightened my resolve to break out on my own, so that when Jim and I found Wheatham Farm at Steep, just north of Petersfield, it was not long before we had it signed, sealed and settled. We were lucky in that the owner too wanted a quick sale.

Wheatham Farm is on a hill close to the remarkable set of great natural ravines which have become known locally as Little Switzerland. Past the edge of these immense wooded gullies, chopped out of the otherwise undulating Hampshire countryside, runs the road to Alton via hairpin bends, where you can look over a sheer drop down into the trees hundreds of feet below. Only a few miles north of Wheatham Farm lies Selborne, made famous by the Reverend Gilbert White in his book *The Natural History of Selborne*. It was certainly a lovely piece of country that we wished to farm in.

In April, much to my father's disapproval, I took all my horses to Steep except for the one owned by the Dunning family which was Smoke Drift – my father would not let me take that. All the others belonged to other people, so he had no hold over those and I took all the horses and my few personal possessions and moved to the farm. Then after I had spent a month or so getting settled Pam moved down with me to help get a house we were acquiring ready and decorated.

Pam and I got married in the September and things went reasonably well at the farm for the first couple of months. In fact everything seemed great until Christmas, when Pam naturally wanted to go home and of course I wanted to go with her. However Jim had other ideas as he wanted me to stay over the Christmas to manage the farm. However I had done all that had to be done, like getting the men's rotas fixed, and as I had not had any time off at all I decided that I was going to have Christmas off.

We had a few words over that and it showed cracks in my relationship with Jim. As a consequence I began to formulate plans to build up another business on my own, training and dealing in show jumpers. I had been doing an awful lot of training while at Wheatham Farm and there had been a good number of horses and people coming to stay with me over the summer to be schooled and given instruction. It seemed to me that rather than play second fiddle to someone else, however well you might get on with them, it would be preferable to be a professional trainer cum show jumper and have students to stay at a yard of my own. It would be much more satisfactory than the present arrangement, and I would at last be my own boss.

When I married her Pam had been a great point-to-point rider. She was highly successful in this field and she was the leading point-to-point rider in the Midlands. The first winter we were married, although she was not then actually riding horses, she still had her heart and soul in point-to-pointing.

For those who do not know, point-to-point is a kind of scaled-down Grand National which is run over a course no less than three miles long and with at least eighteen fences, whose heights used to be around four feet, but have now gone up to four feet three inches. So this is no easy sport, but it is one where women can compete on equal terms with men although 'ladies' races' are always included on the card. The point-to-point was originally what it says, a race from A to B across country, with no one allowed to open any gates, so that you had to go over the hedges and ditches willy-nilly. Nowadays you cannot compete in a point-to-point race unless you have hunted your horse, which is usually a thoroughbred, at least ten times in the previous winter. Point-to-point races are put on between February and May and they are one branch of this kind of sport which started off back in the middle of the last century. The other branch is steeple-chasing, which got into great disrepute at one time, but point-to-pointing was regularized and has become a training ground for jockeys and also a breeding ground for some pretty well-known race horses. One of these was Limber Hill, who won the Cheltenham Gold Cup in 1956.

Point-to-point meetings today are places where you can really get near the horses and riders, and where you can wander about at will to see it all and perhaps put the odd wager on a horse, but the riders are amateurs and can never expect to win more than about forty quid for their efforts. Girls like Pam do it for the fun and the thrill of a chase over hurdles, though I can tell you it scares the pants off me.

Anyway, despite her life having been in point-to-point, Pam decided that now we were married and so that we could spend more time together she would foresake the 'hunt' world and come over to show jumping.

I didn't quite know what I was starting when I began to spend a lot of time giving her the benefit of my experience in show jumping and how to ride the show jump fence. It is a different technique altogether, and one where the mad gallop and the leaping over and through the brush of the hurdles has to be replaced by a relatively slow, controlled pace and a precision which really has little place in point-to-point.

Now my wife was born under the sign of Virgo and that, I'm told, makes her a perfectionist – someone with the kind of mind that catalogues all the facts and stores them a bit like a computer. Pam showed me this side of her nature as we worked together to get her ready for the husband and wife double act of Lionel and Pam Dunning. She was a very talented rider before she married me, but with two heads put together and with her careful and considerate understanding of horses, she developed that fantastic style and technique which has raised her to be one of the leading lady riders in Europe today.

When spring came Harvey Smith, Johnny Greenwood and I went off on the jumping circuit and then went on to Dortmund for an unofficial international opener to the season. When I got home from Dortmund I was met by a very, very unhappy wife indeed. She hated the place, didn't like the house and was not getting on at all well with Jim. She made no bones about it. She was very unhappy and wanted to get away from Wheatham Farm.

So I decided there and then to hell with it, we just had to move. To make matters worse Pam's father was very ill, desperately ill in fact, and he had to go for an operation. Ill as he was I managed to get a message to him over the phone and with that I went straight back into the office and had a straight talk with Jim Byford and told him why I felt I had to get out. Whereupon he paid me out the money I had put into the farm. It was not a vast sum but it was enough to be going on with.

Luckily Pam's parents had managed to acquire a bungalow for us just up the road from them in Brant Broughton in Lincolnshire. We arranged to move in there and I would take over the stables that were attached to Pam's parents' house. With that I got several of my mates together who had lorries and we loaded up the horses and took them the 200 miles to Lincolnshire. We had our caravan and Pam's parents' caravan and were able to pack a good deal of our stuff into them. The caravan convoy likewise went up to Lincolnshire.

Amazingly, now I look back on it, I arrived home from Dortmund at eight on the Tuesday morning and by Wednesday night we had moved lock, stock and barrel to the village where we still live and have our yard today.

Things were really on the move for the Dunnings just then because no sooner had we got into our bungalow, and were not in the slightest bit straight, when, lo and behold, the phone rang and it was the BSJA on the line telling me that I had been selected for the British team to go to Nice. This was to be my first official international. So hardly had we unloaded the lorry and the caravan, but we were loading them up again to go to the South of France. However, in the end I went in Johnny Kidd's lorry as he had some spare capacity, but even so Pam must have wondered whether being a show jumper's wife was such a good idea . . . when no sooner had you moved than you were left 'widowed' again by the call to jump for Britain.

So that, by and large, is how I met my wife, and I now realize that no jump-off against the clock could have been more of a hustle than the way we eventually teamed up together. Neither of us had the faintest idea what triumphs and traumas we were to face in the next few years as we struggled to make it to the top of the show jumping tree as a husband and wife team.

# 9  Big Game

The year after I got married everything was happening. I had some good horses to ride, including Arran Blaze, who had come originally from Bob Richards at Liphook in Hampshire, not all that far from Petersfield where I had been farming. He was a little horse by show jumping standards, only 15.2 hands high – a chestnut by Blaze On. Mrs Sommer and Mrs Wood bought him for Mrs Wood's daughter Sally to ride as an event horse, and he proved to be quite successful at local shows round the South of England. However, in 1971 he started refusing and I was sent the horse in July of that year to see if I could get him going again.

I remember that the first show I took him to was the World Ploughing Match Championships early in 1972 and he jumped into first place both days in the B and C event. What this meant was that the horse was only a grade C horse when I took him there, but with his winnings by the end of the meeting he was a grade B. On the third day he came second to Dietmar Ackerman on Streamline against the clock. I knew that here was a horse who could do well for me, and I took him to Hickstead, where he jumped fantastically. Yet hanging over me was the fact that he had been sent to me to be retrained so that he could be sold on. Indeed I was offered a large sum for the horse at Hickstead because of his outstanding performance, but Mrs Sommer and Mrs Wood, bless their hearts, decided not to sell but to let me ride the horse instead.

This was a time when it was really difficult to get into the first few placings in major classes as there were so many good riders and horses about. David Broome, for example, had Ballywillwill, and Harvey Smith had Summertime and a horse called Evan Jones which won the Wills Hickstead Tankard at Easter. It was when Paddy McMahon was getting in the placings with horses from Fred Harthill's Pennwood stables, but Forge Mill had not yet truly begun to make the incredible mark he was eventually to do. However it was the girls who were often stealing the scenes, with Ann Moore consistently winning on the legendary Psalm, although Tuffet was a good second to her in the Wills Grand Prix Bristol Trophy on the Easter Monday.

There were now familiar names coming up through the juniors – names like Debby Johnsey, Sally Mapleson and Jean Germany, who later was a pupil of mine. Also Caroline Bradley, although she was to climb much higher later, was already making a showing with her horse Franco. I have always respected Caroline Bradley's dedication and courage and it was a terrible shock to all of us who had known her when she died so tragically and at such a young age.

I was jumping with Caroline and Ray Howe (who was on Kalkallo Prince) in the Wills Woodbine Stakes at Hickstead again in July. This is a team relay which is the kind of event I enjoy – something with a bit of fun in it – and we were just beaten into second place by Nicky Payne on Merry Widow, Penny Wilson on Oyster and Roland Fernyhough on Calamity Jane. The day before this (Friday) I had been jumping against Paddy and Forge Mill and sharing equal second place with him and Ann Backhouse. This time I had used Tuffet, while in the Woodbine event it was Arran Blaze. It was a fault-and-out competition which Susan Clarke won on Seventy Seven. Susan, who later became Susan Wilde, has never really hit the headlines, yet she was a good rider and I wonder how many more really good riders have never made it to the top simply because they have not had sponsorship or owners behind them, or the luck to get a really top horse, or perhaps the selfless dedication that Caroline Bradley showed, for instance, to the few top horses in her career. You do really have to give up everything else if you are to succeed in the show jumping world, and many people who would have been as good as, or even better than, the ones who have become household names just have not been able to commit themselves so completely. And the situation is getting worse. Horses and their keep are getting more expensive and the road to the top is getting steeper and more full of pitfalls. It could be that in years to come we shall look back on the seventies as the absolute top of the mountain of show jumping success.

I went to Hickstead a lot that year and Arran Blaze was jumping pretty well, so once again we were in the money in a team relay, but this time Ray Howe and I had Ann Moore to help us to victory. That was a particularly significant win for me, as in second place was the German team which included Alwin Schockemöhle on The Robber as well as Lutz Markel on Sir. Both these were top notch horses, especially The Robber – one of the most famous show jumpers of all time.

Immediately following the Hickstead meeting we went off to Northampton for the British Timken Show, and Pam came too. There was some pretty good competition there with Paddy riding Forge Mill and Steve Hadley on Flying Wild. Derek Ricketts had Tyrolean Holiday and Ray Howe was now riding Streamline. I had a really good show and for the first time in a major event Mr Dunning and Mrs Dunning were bracketed together in the winning places. This was in the Dustin Stakes on the Saturday, when Malcolm Pyrah on John's Venture beat me into second place on Arran Blaze, and I just pipped Pam who got third on Highlander.

However, I won the Popular event on Tuffet that day, beating Derek Ricketts on Elijah. Actually Derek was pretty mad at Tuffet and me after the Timken Show, because while he jumped every fence perfectly clear, Tuffet, who had had clean white bandages put on by my groom before the event, came back with those bandages covered in all the colours of the rainbow from the fences we had hit (but not knocked down) on the way round to beat him into third place! Tuffet was never a very careful horse and it is a wonder that we had as much success as we did.

After that I went on to get second to Paddy on Forge Mill in the oddly named British Show Jumping Association's Olympic Trial, with Derek third on Tyrolean Holiday. It might seem strange that the Olympic squad had already gone to Munich by the time the Olympic Trial was run. However, it lived up to its name, with fourteen massive Olympic-style fences to contend with, and it is simply a matter of form that at every British Timken Show, which incidentally is one of the best shows in the country, there is always an Olympic Trial event. That year, however, it did not quite coincide with the Olympic arrangements.

We had sent Mike Saywell, Harvey Smith, David Broome and Ann Moore to the Olympics, although there was some controversy about the absence of Pennwood Forge Mill, who, on the form he had consistently shown through the pre-Olympic shows, should have gone. How he would have fared over Micky Brinkmann's courses you cannot say, but Ann Moore, so consistent and successful at home, had some unhappy problems in the Grand Prix des Nations with the gallant Psalm in the rough, tough Olympic stadium, but still gained the individual silver. Britain ended up in fourth place behind Italy, with the Germans and the Americans fighting it out for first place and the Germans eventually winning on their home ground, but amazingly by a tiny quarter of a time fault. It didn't really seem fair, seeing that Bill Steinkraus jumped the only clear in the first round* and Neil Shapiro on Sloopy the only clear in the second round, but it was Neil's bad luck to have picked up that damning time fault in the first round when he also had a couple of poles off.

That September we were not jumping at Hickstead because we were in South Africa. In the party was Johnny Greenwood, who in those days was riding Mr Punch, Malcolm Pyrah, Ted Edgar, Pam and me. Johnny Kidd was originally going, but it didn't take much persuading on my part to let Pam and me go in his place, and as well as the English team there was an Irish team. Of course we could not take our own horses, so we were loaned mounts; I was lucky to be given the best one and won the first event of the several shows that we jumped out there.

The Irish contingent included Eddie Macken and Tony Vance. Iris Kellett was the Irish *chef d'équipe*, and one evening a South African lady took Miss Kellett on one side and suggested to her that Ted Edgar was sabotaging the Irish contingent by every night taking them out to all hours and getting them the worse for wear with drink. At this Iris Kellett got really mad, and next morning she had her Irish boys on the carpet about their late-night binges. She insisted that for the rest of the show

*There was one other clear in the first round, which was clocked up by Llambi Jorge of Argentina on Okay Amigo. However, Argentina finished eighth.

they were to be in bed by ten o'clock. Now can you imagine making that kind of ultimatum to Irish lads in their late teens and early twenties and getting away with it? So of course when she came round like a kind of Florence Nightingale to see that they were all in bed, they all feigned sleep, but as soon as they thought she was out of the way they all got up and went out on the tiles again. In fact one particular night Eddie was so far gone that he fell backwards over the seat he was sitting on and had to be doctored up next day so that he could ride his horse. As far as I know, Iris never found out.

After it was all over they took us up to Kruger Park, the big game reserve, and I was really looking forward to this because I envisaged it would be like Treetops, where Princess Elizabeth was staying when she first heard that her father had died and that she had become Queen. However, it was rather more primitive than that and at first I was, to say the least, rather disappointed. Pam on the other hand thought it was marvellous from the word go, and by the end of our stay I had also come around to the same conclusion. It was not Treetops, but it was an experience that I shall never forget. Certainly some unforgettable things happened.

We had the chance to go on a sort of safari at the Kruger Game Park and that was really exciting. It also caused some funny problems. The accommodation is in a sort of kraal, with dozens of little huts with thatched roofs all arranged in ever increasing circles. Well one evening we met Andrew Fenton, who was Johnny Greenwood's groom, and he couldn't remember the number of his hut. He had been wandering round for an age, like someone lost in a maze, trying desperately to find it. I still don't know whether he found it that night or not. I hope he did, because it was intensely dark there when the sun had gone down and I myself fell down a ditch in the pitch black one night.

Another very funny thing happened and this was due to the Irish boys who were more than usually unruly – mainly because they were trying to make up for being seen into bed so early. Anyway, we had a bus-driver who took us out on trips into the bush and he was a bit of a nut-case. He used to put meat out near the edge of the perimeter fence in order to attract the lions at night. This particular night the ladies, including Iris

Kellett, sat down on their chairs about a hundred yards from the wire, hoping to see a lion. Between the huts and the wire there was a large stretch of gravel.

Suddenly, as the ladies sat apprehensively waiting for a lion to appear on the far, safe, side of the wire, there was a growling noise just near them inside the compound and something large jumped on to the gravel. Not waiting to find out what it might be, the ladies screamed and took to their heels as fast as they could go back towards the huts and safety. The 'lion' that had got into the compound was of course one of the Irish lads, and Eddie tells me that one South African lady was so scared that she failed to let go of her chair and scampered off with it still clutched tightly to her as she ran half-bent for safety.

There was another really interesting event we went to that year and that was jumping on a frozen lake at the Swiss ski-resort of Davos. This is one of the most famous winter sports resorts in Switzerland, and is over 5,000 feet up. Amongst its attractions it lists international ski-jumping, ice hockey and exhibition skating. It also has horse racing, riding and horse shows, and it was one of these that we went to. I had Chane Link there and Pam had November Song; she was leading lady rider and I was leading male rider at that show. We had to have five studs put in each shoe to grip the ice plus each hoof packed with water-pump grease to stop the snow balling up. It snowed heavily the first day and after that they covered the surface with three-inch layers of fresh snow each day. It was after this fascinating show that I made one of the biggest mistakes of my life – and a very expensive one – by taking Chane Link to Dortmund and over-facing her over one of Micky Brinkmann's massive courses. After that she really broke her heart and just didn't want to know. She had given everything she had, and I had demanded too much. I learned a great deal from that failure, and I have always been much more careful not to over-face my horses since then.

Anyway, at Davos I did another silly and expensive thing. This was Pam's first show abroad with our own horses and while she was a fantastic event rider I couldn't imagine her doing too well in the international show jumping world, especially on ice. So I said to her, 'Well, do your best and whatever you win you can keep', thinking that I had nothing to lose on that deal. Anyway I figured that even if Pam did win anything they wouldn't pay her out until the Saturday when all the shops – and they have some pretty expensive shops in Davos – were closed. As it was she was second in the first class she entered on the first day and they payed her out in cash. She won several other classes or was placed in them and so she ended up with a lot of ready cash and was off round the shops enjoying herself. It was the first and last time I ever made such a silly mistake, and since then the winnings have been pooled!

After we came back from South Africa I was back in the hunt at the Horse of the Year Show, winning the Dick Turpin Stakes on Chane Link, with Alwin Schockemöhle second and Derek Ricketts third. As well as that I won the Evening News Knockout, again on Chane Link, but this time it was Alwin's brother Paul whom I knocked into second place. I also got a second to Hendrik Snoek who was riding Shirokko in the Country Life and Riding Cup. Chane Link was a really fantastic horse for me at that time and as I think back it makes me more and more sad that I blew her mind at Dortmund so very soon after the Horse of the Year Show.

The Nice experience mentioned at the end of chapter 8 was great for me. It was my second international at Nice as I had been there the previous year (1971) for what had been my first ever international. Anyway this year we beat the French into second place on their home ground, despite some wonderful riding by Pierre Durand on his ex-Olympic horse Pitou. Pitou had won the individual gold at Mexico in the three-day event back in 1968 and so was a horse well known for his bravery and ability. He needed both those qualities on the course they built in the Palais des Expositions. It made getting clear rounds very difficult, so difficult indeed that the only one to jump a double clear was Durand on Pitou.

I didn't do too well in the first round, collecting twelve faults over the thirteen fences which included a double, a treble and a water jump. However Arran Blaze was, I thought, doing well. You get to feel how a horse is performing. OK, he may drop the odd pole, but you somehow know that he and you are both coming good together.

Anyway poor old Pierre was badly let down by his compatriots, and as I was able to discard my cricket score we ended up ahead of Portugal (who were making a come-back into top class international jumping at that time) by six and a quarter faults. All we had was a single quarter of a time fault which came via Stephen Hadley's almost too careful round. Steve is a great craftsman when it comes to jumping and he always works it all out in a scientific manner. He is one of the most technically minded show jumpers I know, as is apparent from the brilliant way in which he analyses the courses when he is commentating on television.

When it came to the second round the French were well down the table, lying fifth of the six teams, but then they staged a come-back. The cheers from all the French supporters when their own side began to pull up with a great clear opener by Pitou was deafening – that is another of the pressures that you have to work against when jumping in an international. Somehow I managed to rise to the occasion and, with my heart thumping with the tension, the exertion and the thrill, I coaxed Arran Blaze over all the fences and we came home clear! It was not quite my first clear round in an international, but I was on fire with pleasure and the congratulations of the rest of the team. As well as Steve Hadley, our team comprised that great veteran Peter Robeson on his equally experienced Grebe and Simon Rodgerson on his grey mare Savannah. As well as us four, Johnny Kidd was there taking part as an individual.

So after my clear, Simon getting four faults and Steve taking it easy and getting a fence down plus a fault and three-quarters as a time penalty, we ended up the winners with a total of only ten faults while the French in second place had nineteen or so. After them came Spain with twenty, while the Portuguese, who had shown up so well in the first round, collapsed to fourth and the Italians were nowhere at all. They said that we were a 'scratch' side, but compared to the Italians on this occasion we were in the top flight.

Better things were to come because my good showing in the Nations Cup fired me on to greater efforts. The Grand Prix de France is run in two parts. There is individual showing in a round against the clock, plus a puissance. I had a great round against the clock and Arran Blaze was really coming good. In the puissance Steve on Freeman just beat me, but I ended up equal second with Marcel Rozier of France. Anyway, what can you do against a horse that is called Quo Vadis?

If that was not enough to make me feel really good, I managed to get fourth in the show championship, with Simon coming second. It was a terrific show for me and coming as it did all mixed up with our move up to Lincolnshire from Petersfield, and with me hardly having had time to draw breath before I was off to Nice, it certainly proved to me that despite all the pressures I could make a showing in the international scene. Gone was the rather amateurish approach of the international meeting in Berlin when I took my father because he wanted to go, with all the hassle that that entailed, and with the long hours at the wheel draining my ability to compete. Here it seemed to me I might at last be on my way to being recognized as a force in show jumping.

Britain won the President's Cup in 1972 and I felt that I contributed to that victory because not only did I ride in Nice at the start of the season, but I was also included in the squad that went to Madrid.

Actually it was all a bit of a farce, because the course-builder they had was not quite up to the job of testing international riders and he built such a low course that after the first round four of the five nations taking part were level peggings, all their members having jumped clears. Only the poor old Portuguese, who hadn't done too badly in Nice for example, were down the drain with fifteen and a quarter faults. The home team were really down on their luck when their star rider Alfonso Segovia was taken ill and so when the officials realized that they were going to have to build the course up for the second round, Spain had only a three-horse entry. They only knocked off a couple of poles and Italy knocked off just one, but in these novice conditions that was enough as both our team and the French were still on a complete set of clear rounds. I had Arran Blaze again and he was proving very consistent. Once again Peter Robeson was there as 'father' of the party, with Ann Backhouse on Cardinal and Alison Dawes with her famous The Maverick.

Because of the dead heat Britain and France jumped off, but

this time they managed to mismeasure the course and even if you galloped flat out there was no way you could get round that course without incurring time faults. It was a horse called Thot, ridden by Jérôme Chabrol, that let us in very easily by managing to clock up no fewer than twenty-eight and a quarter faults when he made a total disaster of riding the combination. Ann Backhouse followed this with a clear round in the best time against the impossible time allowed. All I had to do was to coax Arran Blaze round, and while we had one pole off and the inevitable couple of time faults, we had done all that was needed to put Britain once again on the road to gaining the coveted President's Cup. In case you are not aware of it, let me tell you that the President's Cup is the World Team Championship and is based on each country's best six Nations Cup results. At that time we had either won it or been runners-up seven times out of the previous eight years. We won it in 1965, 1967, 1970 and 1972, and here we were again winning it in 1973.

It is worth noting that you can often do just as well financially by coming consistently in the runners-up places in major classes, or even lesser classes, than you can if you occasionally hit the headlines with a great and spectacular win. I have always been like that, pegging away at all the events I could get into, allowing for horses needing rests and other factors like clashes or accidents. If you look at the published records of the Horse of the Year Show for 1972 as they appeared in the *Horse and Rider Review*, then you will find Lionel Dunning's name just once when he won the Horse and Hound Cup on Bonnie Alice; yet I won the coveted Wembley Spurs that year for the highest aggregate of points scored during the week.

# 10 The Middle Seventies

I had some good wins in 1974 and in April I was riding a new horse that Mr Hartley had bought called Fanny Hill. I spent the best part of a month bringing this horse on, and then at the Royal Windsor in May she took me into the money in more than one major class. In the Thibenzole Stakes she gained me third place behind Harvey Smith on Volvo and Ted Edgar on Everest Jumbo. With a new horse largely untried against this kind of field, this got me off to a good start, and when it came to the massive fourteen-fence Equizole St George of England Stakes I was one of the fifteen clear in the first round. Malcolm Pyrah was riding two horses in this class, his famous Law Court and Trevarrion. Malcolm had won this event the previous year and so was intent on winning it again. However he got drawn with his two horses to start the jump-off against the clock one after the other as first and second horses. On Trevarrion he set a standard of just under fifty seconds, but carelessly dropped a fence. He managed to knock a second off that time on Law Court and went clear. If I was to win this event I had to pull out all the stops. Fanny Hill really went great guns round that big course and was no less than three seconds faster than Law Court, but she just dropped a pole and so we had to be content with second place. However, as far as I was concerned it was as good as a win.

Here's how I came by the fiery Fanny Hill. When Malcolm Pyrah and Judy Boulter decided to get married they needed money, and Malcolm said that Fanny Hill had to be sold. I had a client called Roy Vaughan, who runs a car firm and whose business includes the car parks at Gatwick. He wanted to buy the mare for his daughter Lindsay Vaughan. Lindsay jumped Fanny Hill with only moderate success through 1973, although she did win the Junior International Trial at the Bath and West Show in June. Then at the end of 1973 or beginning of 1974 she was sold to Raymond Fenwick for his daughter Ann to ride. Now Ann had had fantastic success with a very good horse called Brother Dominic, and Raymond therefore thought it worth buying her another good horse. The first show they went to was Cookham where Fanny Hill ran off with Ann, turned upside down and gave her a very bad fall; as she came out of the ring, Mr Fenwick is quoted as saying, 'I'll sell the damned thing – I don't want to see it around.' My owner at that time, Mr Hartley, was also a friend of Mr Fenwick's and there and then in the collecting ring he bought Fanny Hill for me, subject to Pam and I liking her. And that was how I acquired Fanny Hill.

At the Windsor Horse Show that year Mr Hartley had come especially to see Fanny Hill jump. Just as the six-bar competition started he was called away to examine a horse that had had an injury, and when I later went into the ring to collect my rosette and the lovely trophy, poor Mr Hartley was just arriving back on the show ground, having missed the very thing he had come to see!

A six-bar competition is six absolutely vertical fences arranged in a straight line. They are usually painted white, and rather than a mass of poles to make the uprights there are one or two top poles and the space below is filled with a diagonally placed pole. You start off low and gradually work up in height along the line, with each succeeding fence being six inches higher than the one before. So it is rather like a puissance in a straight line but with only two strides between each fence and the next. Fanny Hill won at Windsor with the final fence at six feet six inches high. It can go very high indeed, and in fact Pam won the six-bar at Windsor last year (1983) on Ona Promise with the final fence standing at six feet ten inches, though allowing for the mud the fence was the equivalent of over seven feet.

My first international of 1974 was the one which was held at La Baule just before the immensely popular Men's World Championship. All the countries wanted to use La Baule as a warm-up for the championship and so no less than seven nations competed. This made the contest last a long, long time and both horses and riders got a bit fretful when asked to hang about too long. The Germans won with some very famous horses like Hans Winkler's Torphy, Hartwig Steenken's Simona and Alwin Schockemöhle's Rex the Robber, though it was his brother Paul on the relatively unknown Agent who clocked up the best score over the two rounds. The Americans were second, with over twice the German faults, and we were a few points behind the Americans.

We had Tony Newbery with his Warwick III who got our best aggregate of four faults in each round. The rest of us – Lady Aileen Fraser on Miniature, Judy Crago on Brevitt Bouncer and myself on Fanny Hill – got totals of three faults in the two rounds.

Fanny Hill was to get me my biggest international win of the season – maybe any season – when we won the Grand Prix at Ostend. Fanny was proving to be not only a very accurate little jumper, but also a horse who could get round clear in faster times than anyone else. Anyway, as well as that great individual victory, I was also instrumental in rescuing the other members of our team from what could have been oblivion. The course was such a vast rambling affair that riders just lost their way half way round. The Belgian rider Herve Daout completely lost the track and was eliminated, while our own Tim Grubb on Arksey did the same but somehow managed to find the track again, so ending up with a clear round but with time faults. Poor Auriole Ferguson tumbled off Freelance when he stopped in the double and ended up with nearly thirty penalty points. So Fanny and I had it all to do when we entered the ring. Yet I needn't have worried, for that accurate horse took me round clear not once, but twice, and the only other one to do that was a member of the victorious French team, Pierre Durand on Varin. No one else out of our four went clear, but by being able to discard Auriole's cricket score and with my zero score for the two rounds we ended up just half a point behind the Belgians who were second.

Incidentally there is an interesting story concerning my second round. After the team disaster in the first round and the almost complete disaster of my fellow riders in the second round, Fanny Hill's owner, Mr Hartley, decided that she shouldn't be asked to jump again. However, the British *chef d'équipe* wanted us to go again, and as the commentator was calling for Lionel Dunning and Fanny Hill to come in and jump their round I was arguing with the *chef d'équipe*, though my loyalties were being strained to the hilt. I didn't want to upset Mr Hartley, but on the other hand you only get a red coat when you have jumped a double clear in a Nations Cup event. I had one clear round and I felt I could get another and so get a coveted red coat. So I persuaded Mr Hartley that I ought to jump again for England and the red coat, which of course I did get.

Not content with that success I also won the individual first prize in the Grand Prix on Fanny. When it came to the Grand Prix only three of us were clear. There was Hughueff Persyn of France on the rather unfortunately named Pschitt, but he had a fence down in the jump-off. Then Myrian Thiry on Valse de Vienne rode a careful clear knowing that by doing so whatever happened to me she would end up second. So all I had to do was to ride Fanny Hill accurately and not all that much faster to clinch the Grand Prix title.

The last CSIO of the season was also the first to be held in Austria since the war, and both Pam and I were selected to go. In fact I was outnumbered as a mere male three to one because the other two were Alison Dawes who was riding Tuxedo and Liz Edgar who had Everest Make Do; Pam was riding Sugar Plum.

Liz was the heroine of the party with two clear rounds and Pam followed her closely also with clear rounds, but was just a little slow and so incurred one and a half time faults. Alison dropped two poles in the first round and three in the second while I had one off each time on Tuffet. That put us equal second with the Swiss and only a point and a quarter behind the winners, Germany, who had fielded a strong side. They had Gerd Wiltfang on Firlefanz who got a pole down in the first round, but was clear in the second; Fritz Ligges on Tronfolger, who got a double clear to equal Liz Edgar's total of zero; Herman Shridde on Kadett, who dropped a pole both rounds; and Hans Winkler on Torphy, who had the same score as Gerd. Incidentally Pam had worked wonders with Sugar Plum, who had been discarded by David Broome's stable but taken on by her.

We acquired Sugar Plum this way. One day David Broome rang to say that he had a horse that he thought would suit my wife. It was not big enough for him to ride, and he didn't think it had enough scope to win any big classes. So with that David sent the horse to me, mentioning a certain lowish price. At the time we were on our benders for money and to buy horses even at that price was almost impossible for us. Pam played about with the horse all winter and then we went to Hertogenbosch Horse Show in the spring. As Pam entered the ring in the first class on the first day David came up, put his hand on my shoulder and said: 'She'll break her bloody neck on that animal.' 'Well,' I said, 'she has great faith in the mare and she thinks a lot of it and I am sure she will come out of it OK.' Far from breaking her neck on Sugar Plum, Pam jumped a clear round on her, and when she had just completed that triumph I looked up at David and asked him how much money he now wanted for his mare. I have always admired David because, although he confided that he wanted to make a certain sum on the sale, when I made a clean breast of how things were and that we couldn't afford that amount at that time, he said, 'Well you have her and pay me when you can afford it.'

By the end of that show Lutz Merckel was pestering David to buy the animal, as he was quite a small fellow and Sugar Plum would have been just right for him, especially seeing the way Pam was jumping her into top places in the classes she entered. But David was as straight as a die. 'If you want the mare you have to go to the Dunnings,' he said. 'They own Sugar Plum now.' Yet at that show she was registered as belonging to D. Broome, so he could have sold her and made a handsome profit; however he had promised the mare to us and he stuck to his bargain. This is pretty typical of David, who has always to my mind been a very straight and honest fellow, as well as someone who has always considered his horses' welfare before his own personal wishes. Often David could have won classes where the going was getting rough for the horses, but so often he has withdrawn rather than ask too much of them.

Back in England in the summer we had some good shows. The South of England in early June coincided with the Royal

Cornwall, so it was a toss-up who went where. Ardingly, in Sussex, where the South of England Show is held, was always good territory for me and that year was no exception because I won two of the major classes. I had won the Dunhill Trophy the previous year and I won it again, this time making quite sure of it by coming both first and second on Sporting Award and Bonnie Alice respectively. These two horses were owned by Mrs June Sommer and Mrs Laury Wood.

When Pam and I got married, Mr Hartley was my main owner, but he was limited financially and couldn't afford to supply me with a lot of horses. I had known Mrs Sommer and Mrs Wood for many years. Mrs Wood was the wife of Ken Wood of the Kenwood mixer firm, and Mrs Sommer was the daughter of the boss of Marley Tiles. So I went to them. They owned Arran Blaze as an eventer and I turned him into a show jumper. However, I also managed to persuade them to provide the money to buy Bonnie Alice and Sporting Award.

In the Corrall Championship, still at Ardingly, I once again rode Fanny Hill into first place, with David Broome second on Heatwave. I was pleased to have my old teacher George Hobbs in both third and fourth places, although only David and I got a clear round in the jump-off. George should not have been there if he had listened to his doctors. He had had a slight stroke earlier in the year and had been advised against competing, but keeping George out of the saddle was like keeping a ferret in a marzipan cage – rather impossible. It was my up-and-coming Fanny Hill who jumped a clean and fast clear round to pip David, although it wasn't the fastest time. That was clocked up by the 'invalid' George Hobbs on War Lord. My feelings were mixed there. If George had gone clear he'd have won the event which I was rather pleased to win, but even so I would have liked to have seen him win it to say yah-boo to the medics who wanted to wrap him in cotton wool.

To round off a good show for me, Fanny Hill was only just pipped into second place in the other major class at the South of England – the Blue Circle Stakes. The winner was a bit of a surprise because Mrs Mannie Beavan's nine-year-old Anzac was not in the habit of beating the international field, but she had had the sense to get some experience on the Continent, which stood her in good stead in the event, and Anzac beat us all with the only clear round of the class.

My early success with Fanny Hill made me envisage all kinds of great things for the future, but while I jumped away the summer on her both at home and abroad, what I didn't know was that it was not to be. Just a week later than the Ardingly Show we were at the Essex County Show and Fanny was unbeatable. Here was a combination with which I really clicked – one of those rare link-ups such as Ann Moore and Psalm or Paddy and Forge Mill or Caroline Bradley and Marius. Were we destined to go to the top of the tree? It looked like it when we won the Essex County Championship and the Britvic Trophy – the two major classes at the show. Fanny was no less than eleven whole seconds faster round the championship course in the jump-off than the next horse, which was Rossmore, ridden by John Palmer. She was one of the only two clears in the Britvic and beat the other by two and a half seconds.

On my home ground at the Lincoln County, Sporting Award got me into third place in the Ross Food Stakes, which was the Lincolnshire international trial event. Caroline Bradley was first on Acrobat and also second on Middle Road; this was a time when Caroline's star was in the ascendant and she was winning classes everywhere, so I was not too unhappy with the result.

The British Jumping Derby is a great spectator event with its set-piece fences, including the massive Derby Bank and the sunken Devil's Dyke which, if you do not get a helluva lot of impulsion and keep your rhythm and momentum going right through it, can be a real trap. Whenever I rode Tuffet in this event we never finished lower than fifth. But this particular year I rode Fanny and did well on her. It was the year that Harvey became the first man to win the Derby three times. Fanny took me clear almost all the way round: we negotiated the Bank and the Devil's Dyke as well as the water jump without any problems, which left just the last fence, but as so often happens that last fence was the one we clobbered. They said I was 'unlucky' to have that fence down just as they said Alwin Schockemöhle was unlucky when Talisman stopped at the stockade fence. Yet I bet Alwin's disappointment did not match mine because when you think you have it all sewn up and you have ridden a really fine round, to have the last down is really upsetting. What's worse, you cannot give vent to your feelings with a television camera lens looking straight into your face.

There was a jinx broken that year. It had become apparent that no one who had won the Derby Trial had ever won the Derby itself, but Hendrik Snoek on Shirokko won the Trial this time, with Eddie Macken second on Pele and Talisman third. Hendrik had won the Derby two years earlier, when Paddy was second on Forge Mill and Derek Ricketts third on Tyrolean Holiday. So Snoekey had now won both. It remained only for someone to do the thing properly by winning both the Trial and the Derby at one meeting.

Still I had a good win in a major class, again with Fanny, when I shared the first spot in the Wills Embassy Grand Stakes with George Hobbs (riding War Lord), beating Harvey Smith on Harvest Gold into third place. It was a good feeling that I, who had once been the pupil, was now equal to the master, and that the two of us should share the honours and the spoils. There was no one with whom I would rather have ridden out to the presentation of awards than George, and I think he felt the same about me.

Since Fanny Hill I have never had what I would call a perfect Derby horse. Others have had them and some still have them. Horses like Deister, which Paul Schockemöhle has ridden with such success for the past years, Eddie Macken's Boomerang and Harvey Smith's Matty Brown and Salvador, John Whitaker's Ryan's Son. . . . Horses like these are very level-headed, and when they get to the top of that bank they pause and think before they launch down the precipitous side of that very dangerous slope, made more difficult by having a fence within a stride or two of the bottom. It is also a question of the kind of horse that clicks with your own temperament. I always have and like horses that are a bit hot, so they will win me money, not by coming first in a few events but by finishing consistently in second, third and even lower places. This way the prize money mounts up, but you do not overtax your horses and do not burn them out rapidly, as happens with some of the top-flight headline-stealers in the game.

Only a fortnight after the Derby meeting the show jumpers were back at Hickstead for the September show, but some of the big names were missing as they had gone off to the prestigious show at Aachen. This enabled a bright young rider, Pip Nichols, on his eleven-year-old Timmie, to win the big class of the meeting – the W.D. and H.O. Wills British Championship. Pip was just seventeen at the time, and he had already put some kind of a stamp on the meeting by getting third in the Young Rider's Championship the day before. Timmie had been one of Liz Edgar's string, but I had a bond with Pip since he was a pupil of George Hobbs, just as I had been.

In fact Pip had been under George's wing for some five years, and the experience had obviously done him good, just as it had me, because when given a good mount and a chance he was able to take it and so beat great names like Harvey Smith and Eddie Macken into second and third places in this top event. Actually Pip Nichols came on to me for tuition all that year, and so the close-knit bond with George Hobbs still continued.

Autumn is often sad, but that September was one of the saddest ever, as I lamed Fanny Hill. We took her to compete in the show jumping events that are run in conjunction with the World Three Day Event at Burghley, where she slipped at a fence and a pole caught her behind the knee and ricked her tendon very badly. She didn't break down as such, except that she did have a bit of a leg. Fanny had always been a mare that had suffered with brucellosis, which leads to extremely swollen joints or tendon sheaths. It was this condition that contributed to Fanny Hill's very swollen leg. This kept her off all work for a good three months, and in fact she was off show jumping until the following year when I took her to Geneva. While we were there Ronnie Masserella, the British *chef d'équipe*, pleaded with me to go to Rome, and it was in Rome in the very first competition that Fanny Hill broke down. She never jumped again.

The year 1975 opened with a bang for me when I had some real fun leading the show jumpers' entry to the Hickstead Easter cross-country. The weather was so appalling that

Douggy Bunn decided that he was not going to risk the main jumping events in the International Arena. That left us, to coin a phrase, high and dry, and we were all frustrated and raring to have a go at anything.

I had never taken part in a cross-country in my life – that was Pam's scene – but Ted Edgar managed to persuade Ray Howe, Steve Hadley, Bob Ellis and me to risk our necks over the waterlogged mile-and-a-half course. Actually it was a very dicey do altogether and there were many who said it should never have been allowed to run, but run it did, despite one horse of the team that led off having to be put down when it broke its neck at only the second fence. There have to be five members in a team, of which four have to finish, and just before we set off on this escapade Ted, who as I say had set the whole ball rolling, came up to the practice hedge and managed to lame his horse. I was OK, as I had Pam behind me telling me exactly how to ride these hedges and ditches at speed, because that was her great thing, but poor Ted had no horse to ride, and anyway the whole entry would have to scratch if we didn't have five starters.

Well, as luck would have it, help arrived in the shape of a very American voice which said, from behind a hedge, 'Gee, man, I'd just love you to ride my horse.' The owner of the voice was a very small man and the horse he was offering Ted was no more than fifteen hands. Ted looks at this little horse and says, 'Well, it'll never carry me.'

'Oh yes, man, it will,' came back the reply. 'It's a very good jumper and I've come down here hoping that I would be able to join a team, but there haven't been any takers so please, please, ride my horse.'

So it was that Ted rode this little horse at speed and in the atrocious conditions all the way round that cross-country – and finished, just as we all did. There were a few spills, but until two minutes before the start Ted had never sat on his mount. He had one jump over the practice hedge and then we were off, having to ride with the utmost care in order to meet the fences and ditches just right, so as not to slither and slide about. The discipline of riding your horse on a perfect stride into each fence pays off whatever you are doing, and so despite my four fellow

99

stalwarts all coming off at various times we won the event. In this cross-country four have to finish and the time is from when you start to when the fourth member of the team is through the finish. It was a bit slow for me as I managed to stay on all the way round, but had to hang on while the others remounted. We thought it was a pretty good win, seeing that it was the Royal Artillery team that was second and the Mid-Surrey Draghounds third. All these people were experienced cross-country riders and we were just plain show jumpers – but every one of us finished and it was a great victory.

Without my great hope Fanny Hill it was May before Arran Blaze got me back into the top three of major classes, when we managed two thirds at the Bath and West. In the Cockburn's Special Reserve Stakes there were just three of us clear at the end of the first round, but not one of us managed it clear in the jump-off. Harvey on Salvador won it with four faults while Graham Fletcher on Buttevant Boy beat me into third place.

We had some of the Harvey Smith shenanigans in the Everest Double Glazing Stakes, which Forge Mill won, with Caroline Bradley second riding Acrobat and myself third again on Arran Blaze.

There were eleven of us clear after the first round. Paddy was first in and jumped clear again, followed by someone else whose name I don't remember. Then came Harvey who decided that the setting of the second part of the double was not right and he made the course-builders change it. However this did not please the judges who said, rightly, that as two horses had already gone, despite Harvey being correct in objecting to the distance, the double had to stay as it was. That made Harvey mad and he flounced out of the ring, but Harvey's temper soon evaporates and just as they were announcing that he had retired he suddenly appeared again to jump his round. Probably because he was fuming inwardly at what he thought was a bungle on the officials' part he had the first part of the double down – not the part he had complained of – and he repeated this mistake when he later rode Harvest Gold. So that was the end of Harvey's chances, and it just goes to show that it is probably better to carry on even if the course is not quite right rather than risk an upsetting confrontation. The judges' decision is in my experience always final. I've rarely known them make an error and admit it publicly.

At the start of the fateful 1976 season I was jumping a very good horse that I had bought in late 1975 called Free Agent. He was a winner of many classes. I was also still riding Arran Blaze and Bonnie Alice, while Pam was riding Miniature and Blue Saffron. This was the year that I bought Union Jack from the Barker twins of Northallerton, and at the same time I was riding horses for John E. Taylor – known as Jet from his initials. He is an owner who has had some famous horses – some of them for instance were ridden by Harvey Smith.

As for Miniature, Sir Hugh Fraser had bought the horse for Aileen, but she wasn't getting on with him very well, and one night Sir Hugh rang me to ask if I would be available to ride the animal, which I was only too pleased at that moment to do. He arrived in time for the Lincolnshire County Show. There I rode him in the AIT and he went disastrously so that I had no less than three fences down and I came out of the ring swearing that I'd never ride the bloody horse again. I didn't like him and he didn't seem to like me; anyway he was too small. So Pam asked if she could ride him and, believe it or not, she jumped straight on to that horse, took him into the next competition and won it! But then Pam is like that. When she clicks with a horse she can coax remarkable performances out of it with very little previous work. She usually does a lot of work on most horses before they get to the way she wants them to be, but when occasion demands she can ride them 'cold' and still do well.

Despite the failure with Miniature at the Lincoln County Area International Trial it was only one of the horses I was riding. The class that was the AIT was the Everest Double Glazing Stakes, and I rode Bonnie Alice into second place behind Tim Grubb's First Time, so I was rather more pleased at the end than I was at the beginning.

While I was 'at home' Pam was off to Scotland to take part in the Highland and then the inaugural Glasgow City Show. There was a lot of sponsorship money at this show, because they wanted to tempt the top riders to stay on north of the border for a few days after the Royal Highland and so get this new Glasgow event off to a good start. The high prize money certainly attracted Harvey, who won the Whyte and Mackay Stakes on Olympic Star, with Graham Fletcher on Tauna Dora second. Pam was riding Oliver Schmitt's Blue Saffron and she shared equal third place with Nick Skelton on Everest OK. Still, as the first prize was £2,000 there was just a little bit for Pam to win, even in an equal third place.

The lady riders were well in evidence because Debby Johnsey, riding her famous Olympic horse Moxy, won the other major class – the Radio Rentals Stakes – with Liz Edgar second on Everest Wallaby. This was the incredibly dry year when the the ground became concrete hard, so that riders who cared for their horses' legs, as David Broome has always done, were to be found leaving major shows very soon after they opened. At the Royal Norfolk, for instance, David went home after the first day because of the hardness of the ground, but not, I might add, before he had shared first prize in the Holden Motor Stakes with Paddy McMahon on Forge Mill.

I had my near-fatal accident on 1 August, and from then on there was no chance of the record books having L. Dunning's name in them; but Pam had to pick herself up and go on competing, which she did, and at Hickstead in the first few days of September she picked up both first and third places in the Embassy Gold Stakes. She got first place on Blue Saffron and third on Sir Hugh Fraser's Miniature, while Vicky Gascoigne made it an all-girls event by getting second place. However, those were not the only top places Pam managed because, despite the competition being very fierce at that time, she jumped Miniature into second place behind Caroline Bradley on Marius in the Lambert and Butler Stakes, with Graham Fletcher on Double Brandy third. Such wins were of great importance to the Dunning partnership just then, and of course they were not the only classes in which Pam was in the prize money, which can go down to tenth place or even lower if the sponsorship money for the class is big.

Our affairs had fallen under a very bad star for, as so often seems to happen, our troubles did not come singly. Only a week after the operation on my damaged shoulder, when I really wanted something to boost my morale, we heard that Mrs Laury Wood had died. That knocked me back even more.

Together with Mrs Sommer, this lady had kept us in horses and had been a good friend as well, and now she was dead. That meant the horses she owned had to be sold, and we lost them, because her family were not at all interested in show jumping, but wanted to realize her estate.

There is a strange tale to tell here. I don't often think of myself as a psychic person – too down to earth for that – but I well remember a very remarkable thing that concerned Laury Wood's death.

It was while I was still in a state of semi-consciousness, due to the drugs and pain-killers I was having to take, that one night I dreamed I was in a graveyard. All of a sudden it came over very, very cold. A mist rose in my dream and covered all the grave stones and with that I was suddenly awake and, glancing at my bedside clock, I remember being quite surprised that it was exactly three o'clock.

Next morning, half way through the morning, I received a phone call. It was Laury Wood's daughter Sally ringing to inform me that her mother had died that morning, but when she added that her mother had passed on at exactly three a.m. I was a bit flabbergasted, because my dream had coincided with the event. Maybe there were reasons for this strange coincidence. Laury had known me ever since I was a babe in arms, and so she had a particularly soft spot for me. Could she possibly have been thinking of me as she died? I often wonder.

While Pam was competing with success at Olympia in 1975, Sir Hugh Fraser invited us into his viewing box and literally gave Miniature to Pam to ride in perpetuity. It was, according to Sir Hugh, never to be sold, but we in return agreed always to jump it under his name. This in the end proved to be a painful and costly gesture.

In the early part of 1976, in fact in January of that year, Sir Hugh went on a gambling spree and lost some two million pounds just like that. So he sold all his horses to Trevor Banks and Mr Banks insisted that, as Miniature was under Sir Hugh's name, the horse was part of the package and would have to come to him. In fact he made it clear that unless Miniature *was* included the deal was off. So Sir Hugh, who would never himself have deprived Pam of her very successful ride, was forced to go back on his promise, and Miniature was lost to us. That is how show jumping goes. Because good proven horses are so difficult to come by, and take so long to bring on to a state where they consistently win the big money, so people often use desperate methods to get them, as we shall find out at the end of this book.

Thus it was that over the Christmas period of 1976 Sir Hugh Fraser came on the phone to say that he was in money problems and he had sold all his horses including Miniature. That was a terrible disappointment, when we had been led to believe that the horse would be with us for ever. However, Sir Hugh was pressured into selling Miniature against his will, and the fact remained that our main money-earning horse for that winter was gone. This, combined with my inability to ride, all but finished us. Could there be any more blows to endure before we hit the bottom of this terrible trough in our affairs?

# 11 Behind the Show Jumping Scenes

In this chapter I am going to let you into some of the secrets of what we get up to when the jumping is over and we want to relax and get rid of the tensions of the day. But let me start at the beginning, with something that happened many years ago now. It was when that great show jumping horse Foxhunter was at his peak. He was ridden by Colonel Harry Llewellyn, who is a legend in the riding world for his prowess with that famous horse.

This incident happened at the Brighton Show. Foxhunter's groom was an old-fashioned boy who always wore breeches and gaiters as they did in the old days. He always held his breeches up with a pair of very thick webbing braces and – I can see it now as if it were yesterday – the old boy led Foxhunter out of his box to a water trough just in front of the stable. While the horse guzzled his water the groom sat down on the trough for a quick smoke and then suddenly there was a scream and a yell from the direction of Foxhunter's stable and the groom was nowhere to be seen. What had happened was that Foxhunter had finished his water, picked up his groom by his braces and carried him straight back into his stable. Which shows just what a character this horse was. It is a known fact that really top horses are just like people. Those which are a bit eccentric and more intelligent than other, more stolid, beings, are the ones who will be the outstanding performers, which of course Foxhunter was.

That happened in the days when I was still in ponies, and I well remember another incident from that era. I was at a show with my father when a certain famous show jumper turned up after dark with his horses and, finding there was no stabling to be had decided something had to be done. The horses couldn't be left in the box all night, so he said to himself, 'Perhaps I'll put the horses in this tent for the night,' and as he couldn't think of any reason why not, he opened up the door of the tent, popped the horses inside and forgot all about them until next morning. The alarm went off very early and he got up to make sure that no one would find his animals in their tent. So it was that he picked and stumbled his way in the darkness before dawn over what he thought were bales of straw and other bits and pieces, caught his horses and put them back on the lorry for their breakfast.

As soon as the showground began to open up a whole group of people arrived at the tent that had served as a stable and all hell was let loose. Everybody who was anybody at the show came to the tent to see what had happened. The Show Secretary arrived, and then the Show Organizer, and then the police were called in, but luckily nobody was able to say who had stabled their horses overnight in one of the prize flower tents on the show ground!

When I first started going to shows there was a talented trainer of show jumpers called Snowey Mitcherson, who was a very colourful character. Now Snowey was up to every trick in the book – you name it, Snowey had done it. I was at a horse show with him once and I went to him and said,

'Mr Mitcherson, I suppose you wouldn't have any food for my horses? I just want to borrow some to tide me over as I'm a bit short.'

'Oh, you don't want to worry about that, Lionel my son,' he says. 'These girls are always overfeeding their horses. So I'll show you what to do. In fact I'll show you how I feed mine.'

So we stood around for a while and then along comes one rich young lady's groom with enormous buckets of food which she tips into the mangers and goes off. With that Snowey picks up his bucket and fills it with half the food from each manger so that he can feed his horses.

'That's fine,' I said. 'But how about mine?'

'Ah, you just hang about,' he said. 'You've got to wait for the next one.' So I had to wait until someone else came along with more than their fair share of horse food. I wouldn't do that today, of course, but at that time, when I was literally penniless, it was a lesson learned in how to survive at a show without any money.

The first time I ever went to Shrivenham Horse Show was in about 1966. This show was held near Swindon, but has now ceased to function. When I got there I found I had four nice stables, and I got my horses into them and bedded them down. Just then along comes Charley Parker, who was a perfectionist when it came to his horses, and he had been given some rather grotty stables for his horses. So it was that there was knock, knock, knock on my lorry door and it was Charley.

'Hey boy,' he says. 'Do you need those good stables?'

So I replied, 'Well I do really Mr Parker.'

That wasn't good enough for him: 'Will you sell them to me?' he says.

'No,' I say. 'I've paid for them.'

'Well,' he replies. 'The ones I've got aren't really good enough for my class horses and I'd rather pay a bit extra and get my horses in better stables.'

With that I thought, 'Ah ha, the starting fees at the show are going to be £30 and I could do with that £30.' Not only that, I didn't actually have £30 and would have to win it before I could pay! So I said, 'OK, Mr Parker, the stables cost me' – and I stated a slightly inflated figure – 'and if you like to give me £30 you can have my four stables.'

'Right young man,' he said, 'thanks very much.' So I put my horses in his grotty stables, where they were as right as rain, and he put his horses in my super deluxe stables. Now I doubt if his horses noticed the difference, but I ended up with my starting fees and was able to keep all my winnings.

It was also at this show that I first met the Edgars. One of Ted's horses had lost a shoe, and as I was also a farrier I was able to reshoe it – and make enough money for my diesel home!

Show grounds are, as far as their organizers are concerned, not available for use by competitors at any times other than the official ones. The course-builders put up their courses, and they may be the same from day to day or the builders may use the same fences in different places. Very often the course for the following day has to be built the previous evening and so is available if anyone can get into it.

Because they have such great difficulty in getting useful practice at shows there are many tales of show jumpers who have got up early, before any of the officials are about, in order to practice over difficult fences. If, for instance, you have a horse who in a previous competition has had a fall, or a stop at a particular fence, then at first light you attempt to get the horse out there to jump that offending fence and hope you do not get caught doing it.

An early morning escape which happened many years ago involved Ray Howe, who had a horse called Balmain. Balmain was a super horse, except that he was a little bit spooky at ditches. In the days before Hickstead was as good as it is now, without the number of stands and the good fencing that it has now, Ray decided to take Balmain down and give him a jump over the water.

So, very early on this particular morning, Ray rode Balmain down to the arena, popped over the fence at the end where the permanent stand is now and proceeded to jump backwards and forwards through and over the water until he was almost satisfied. Just at that moment, however, he saw someone coming across the arena to find out what was going on. In a panic he jumped off, slipped saddle and bridle as he did so, and left the horse to his own devices while he ran off as fast as his legs would carry him until he got to the gate. Then he walked up the Brighton Road with his tack on his arm, in through Douglas Bunn's garden, over his fence and back into the stables. There he put his tack up and, like a good boy, got back into bed. However, if it had not been so murky and if Ray had troubled to look a bit closer, he could have saved himself a lot of trouble and a big fright, because the avenging person coming across the arena was nothing other than a coat with a hat on top left hanging on an upright by one of the officials just by the little hut in the middle of Hickstead's arena.

Then there was the time when the West Country rider Tom Brake was riding the great Liza Wake and he was having some trouble with the horse jumping the water. Liza would not go sharp enough to the take-off tape to clear the far tape and would always hesitate just on take-off. We were at the Royal Show, where Mr Gerald Barnes was clerk of the course and had his caravan parked by the ring. So, because Tom had come to me and said in his rich West Country accent, 'How can we give this 'ere hoss a school?', I went to see Mr Barnes and told him our problem.

'Well,' said Mr Barnes. 'If you get up really early and don't get caught, and above all don't make a lot of noise, then I promise you I won't look out of the window at who's in the arena schooling their horse over the water.' So with that I arranged to come round to dear old Tom's caravan at first light, which I duly did. I banged on the door and a very sleepy voice told me to come in. 'Oh darn it,' says Tom from the depths of his warm bed. 'I'm gettin' too old for this sort of thing. I'm not going to bother. If the bloody horse puts his foot on the tape then that's just hard luck,' and with that he turned over and went to sleep again. I felt a bit fed up, having troubled to get up so early, but I went back to bed as well and thought that was the end of our early morning escapade.

Next morning about ten o'clock or so I met Mr Barnes, who was more than a little annoyed. 'Now look here young man,' he said sternly. 'Why for Pete's sake did you make so much bloody noise this morning when I expressly asked you not to? You made enough noise to wake the blooming dead.' He really told me off, and when I could get a word in edgeways, I said, 'But Mr Barnes, Tom didn't want to get out of bed this morning and we didn't go to the ring in the end.' At that the good judge blew his top, because whoever it was who had been out in that ring at dawn had woken him up good and proper, and he had sat there in his pyjamas making himself a cup of tea and, true to his word, not even glancing out of the window while the early morning jumpers made a great hullabaloo, which any judge worth his salt, and parked by the ring, must have heard. He never did find out who it was, and neither did I!

There may be other 'early morning' stories to be told, but one of the best ones I know happened at the Three Counties Show just after Alan Oliver, one of our great show jumpers of the sixties, had retired and had taken up course-building. He walked into his arena one morning to look at the course he had set and realized at once that someone had been tampering with one of his jumps. It was a combination that was set to be jumped towards the collecting ring and he knew someone had been jumping it because there were the tell-tale hoof marks to prove it. So Alan immediately changed his combination to be identical to the existing one, but this time to be jumped coming *away* from the collecting ring.

Now it is a well-known problem for show jumpers at any level to get their horses to jump combinations with due care and attention, either when they are going towards the collecting ring (which they consider is 'home'), or when coming away from it, as they are reluctant to go away from home. The latter is the more difficult of the two.

So Alan changed his combination round the other way and then sat there watching intently for his special competitor to appear. He was searching for a certain look of consternation on the face of someone as they walked the course and realized that the combination was not as it had been the night before. He thought he had detected his man when a certain famous gentleman came in, and he was sure of it when the person got eliminated at the reversed combination. Then he knew exactly who had been out that previous night training his horse over the combination – but doing it the wrong way!

Talking of combinations reminds me of the time when, at a particular meeting on the Continent, I and another British rider decided that unless we did something drastic we would have no chance of winning the Grand Prix. The Continentals tend to ride their courses faster than we do, and this meant that the distances that were true or correct for them in between the elements of combination obstacles were too long for the British, who jump at a much slower pace. We found that our horses could not cope with these distances and something had to be done about it.

So the night before the Grand Prix we decided that we had to alter this, and went back into the arena after dark. When we got to the treble we found that it was a yard too long both ends, so we moved the two outer fences in by a yard. We must have made a good job of it because the course-builder didn't even notice and indeed never even inspected his precious treble. In fact, as I recall it, he did not even trouble to look at the course he had built the night before at all that next morning. These days most course-builders are aware that their courses may be tampered with during the night and will always check that everything is as it was, but this particular chap was a bit of a greenhorn (or very lazy) and did not bother to recheck the course.

That was lucky for us as one of us won the event and I was second. In those days our horses did not have the ability to cope with long combinations and so we could not have come anywhere near being in the placings if the lengths had been left as they originally were. In any case the treble consisted of three parallels, which is a very hard combination at the best of times, but with the extra lengths in it would have been totally impossible for us.

When Pam and I first got married in 1973 we were joined by Tim Grubb. Tim was a very ambitious rider and wanted to get on in the world. Today he is one of the best riders in the world and although now based in the United States he was selected for the British team for the 1984 Olympics. In those days Tim used to ride a little horse of Mrs Sommer's and Mrs Wood's called Thomas O'Malley and another one called Sais. Then he went in for another horse called Ghengis Khan. Now every time this latter horse saw a coloured pole he would bolt off. So we took it out in the field one particular day and jumped it over some rustic fences and it was perfectly OK. Yet immediately we showed it some coloured ones it began to back off. Now at the bottom of the field there was an electric fence which they had put across where they were widening the river that runs along there. They had taken my fence away and put up an electric fence to stop the cattle I then had going into the river. Ghengis Khan napped and backed and napped and backed until unhappily he touched the electric fence.

Off went the horse, with Tim hanging on for dear life, across the field at full gallop, jumped the paddock fence, through another paddock, over the gate into the orchard (which I have since turned into an all-weather sand school) and then into our yard, which is a long narrow one between the rows of stables. Straight through the yard he galloped and across the road – luckily nothing was coming – and he ended up in the garden of our neighbour Mrs Lloyd-Jones. With that it deposited Tim in the middle of this lady's lawn and did so by tipping him on to Mrs Jones's washing line, where she was drying all her smalls.

It still makes me laugh when I recall the sight of Tim Grubb in the middle of the lawn with Mrs Lloyd-Jones's undies wrapped round his neck. In another way it was not so funny, because poor old Tim cut his eye pretty badly. Because a doctor with whom he was friendly lived next door to Mrs Jones, Tim decided to wait for him to come home to stitch up his eye. That took most of the day, and eventually, when he did get back from his rounds, the doctor said that it was a bigger job than he could handle and sent Tim off to Newark hospital.

Later Tim managed to acquire the job of riding for Ronnie Masserella and rode Arksey and Askan in the British team when we were in Rome. On the morning of the Nations Cup event we were all sitting round sunning ourselves in the exercising arena, which was some two miles from the show ground, when Tim came wandering down. We were eating hamburgers and drinking Coke, and we said to Tim, 'What do you think of the course then?'

Tim raised his eyebrows: 'Course? What course?'

'The Nations Cup course that you have to walk by twelve o'clock,' we replied.

It was by now eleven and Tim didn't quite believe us. 'We have to do what?' he repeated.

'You've got to walk the course,' we said again, and just to reinforce the message Malcolm Pyrah repeated it: 'You've got to walk the course by twelve o'clock, Tim.' Well with that, and in all the Italian heat, Tim ran into the stables, put on all his best riding togs and then ran across a lot of Rome to get to the ring which as I said was two miles away. He walked the course as he thought he ought, but he got a bit uneasy when he found he was the only one actually there.

Meanwhile we continued to bask in the sun, finishing our hamburgers and Cokes and just waiting for Tim to come back, which he eventually did – very hot and flustered. 'My God,' he said breathlessly, 'but it's a biggun.' 'Is it really Tim?' we said. 'Tell us more about it.' Which he proceeded to do at considerable length and then it suddenly dawned on him that maybe he was the victim of a practical joke, which of course he was, as we didn't actually have to walk the course until two o'clock. It was a bit of a dirty trick, I suppose, and Tim was not exactly happy with things. Indeed he was so annoyed with the trick we had played on him that he hardly spoke to any of us for the rest of the day. But he got his own back on us by jumping a double clear on Arksey.

There is a lot of sport that goes on around the show ground that few people ever get to know about. There is a great deal of friendly rivalry and often harmony between riders, and while in the ring it is every man for himself (because it is now a big sport with big money involved), when we let our hair down we forget our public image and become much more human.

Some years ago – it would have been about 1969 or 1970 – at the Suffolk Show, Tom Hudson arrived with his caravan and parked it beside the fence and then went out to have his customary pint – or two. It was Trevor Banks's wicked idea to move Tom's caravan so that the only door was next to the fence and couldn't be opened. Tom arrived back at the ground a little the worse for drink at about half past eleven or twelve and we were all waiting to see what happened, but keeping well out of sight.

Poor Tom, he couldn't for the life of him see how to get back into his caravan and not being quite in command of all his senses he tried and tried to get in, with us all killing ourselves with laughter at his predicament. In the end he gave up and went and asked for a doss down in someone else's caravan who had been down at the local inn.

I remember one incident from the days when Marion Mould and her horse Stroller were at their peak, and riders like Derek Kent were jumping their strings of horses. Derek used to ride for the Parkers in those days and had a wonderful collection of mounts including a horse called Banhar, another called London Town, plus a little mare called Michaila.

One particular day at Hickstead, Derek had been ribbing and teasing George Hobbs and he hadn't left poor George alone all day. It was a very hot day and a couple of times Derek had flung a glass of lemonade over George which, in the circumstances, was not too bad as he dried off quickly.

Now what this was all about I don't really recall, but it went on all day and George didn't retaliate at all, despite this constant tormenting by Derek Kent. Then in the evening George got his own back with a vengeance.

Derek drove a little Fiat car with a sunshine roof, and he was off out with a girl that evening. So he went to his lorry and changed into his best togs. Now George had managed to come by a couple of big barrels, and with the help of his brother Wally had stood them by the gate. Together they had filled them up with water, vowing as they did so that they would 'get that Kenty'. And there they sat, waiting, waiting, waiting – until chuff, chuff, chuff round the corner comes Derek in his little car, looking forward to his evening out.

But he didn't get to his date, because first of all 'click' went the Hickstead gate as it mysteriously shut. Derek of course got out to see why the gate had shut on him, and then he saw George and Wally. He only had time to blurt out, 'What the devil are you doing?' before – 'wham' – there was the first bucket of water and – 'wham, wham' – two more buckets of water, and they didn't stop drenching Derek until the barrels were all but empty. Then they managed to stuff a whole barrel into the car and shut the door. As Derek opened the door all the water comes spilling out and his car was awash as well as himself.

It was certainly a great revenge, which Derek had to take in good part as he had provoked it, but it was his only suit and so his lady friend, whoever she was, got stood up that evening, which really served him right for teasing and pestering poor George Hobbs.

This escapade with the water was a fairly typical one. We are always having water fights and getting each other saturated. This often happens when it has been very hot jumping round the rings during the day and everyone has become a little bit bored. No one ever starts fist fights in show jumping circles – we just drench each other with water to let off steam (or perhaps create it) and settle a few minor scores.

It isn't only the men who get involved in these water fights – the girls do so as well sometimes, and I remember one fight which involved Marion Mould. This particular evening I had half a bucket of water and was chasing Marion. As I was getting too close to Marion for her comfort she, in desperation, opened the door of a caravan and jumped inside. With that there was a scream and a shouting and yelling and the sound of a man swearing, and Marion proceeded at full tilt out of the caravan by the door on the other side while I went in after her. Then there was more swearing and cursing and a helluva commotion from inside the caravan, and I too went tumbling out. Now Marion knew perfectly well whose caravan this was. It was Geoff Bates's, and she jumped in there hoping he would give her refuge. What she didn't know was that at that moment Geoff was having a stand-up bath – and there he was, stark naked in his little galvanized tub. When Marion burst in she was horrified by what she saw and promptly disappeared out of the nearest door. As if it were not enough to have a young lady dashing through his bathroom, Geoff then had to contend with a young man roaring through with half a bucket of water and leaving both doors wide open so that all the world could see him at his ablutions. I didn't live that one down for years.

One year at Hickstead Douglas Bunn was giving a party. I went to it, and was standing at the bar drinking with Aileen Fraser, who was Aileen Ross in those days before she married Sir Hugh Fraser. We drank for a while, and then the music started up so we decided to dance, and we went on dancing through the evening as Aileen didn't seem to have a partner. Eventually I asked her, 'Who were you supposed to come with?' 'Well,' she said, 'I was supposed to meet David Broome, but he has gone to one of these official meetings and he hasn't come back yet.' So we went on dancing and drinking, and eventually David turned up. Although he apologized for being late, poor David cut no ice with Aileen. 'You push off,' she said. 'I've found myself a man for the evening and we're getting on very well.' Not surprisingly, David was a bit unhappy at this rebuff. He stalked off out of the party and we didn't see him again that night.

So in the morning I decided that I ought to make my peace with David, with whom, as I have said elsewhere, I have always been on good terms. So I went round to his caravan to find Monica, his groom (who is now Mrs John Fay and lives in Australia), cooking his breakfast. I opened the conversation by saying something like, 'I'm sorry about last night, David. I really only teamed up with Aileen as she was on her own and so was I. I didn't want it to end up like that.'

'Never mind,' says David with a laugh and a wave of his hand. 'We'll just put it down to experience but – you little bugger – I'll get one back on you one day, don't you worry.'

The season went on and I forgot all about this incident until we all arrived at Shrewsbury Flower Show. On the Friday night Harvey invited everyone to go to the pub and have a drink. While we were having a drink we started to play darts. There was Ted Williams, Harvey Smith, Johnny Cottam, David Broome and myself. It turned out by chance that David and I teamed up, and we were absolute mustard. We just won hands down, with the other riders nowhere. So David said, 'Let's have a game for money, a fiver a game.'

To me that sounded a damned good idea as we were so much better than the other pairs. So off we went, but as soon as we started to play David was absolutely hopeless. He was missing the board all the time, so that we lost the very first game. I said to him, 'What's up with you?'

'Oh I don't know,' he says. 'I've just lost my eye – can't do a thing.' All through the game I continued to play well, but with his rotten score we just had to lose. So I lost my fiver as well, and as I passed over my money David turned to me with a wicked grin on his face. 'Gottcha,' he said triumphantly 'That'll teach you to pinch my girl friend.'

What I hadn't known was that Harvey had cooked up a scheme with David that he (Harvey) and Ted Williams would play very badly for the first few games, so that I became cocky, and then they would play properly while David played abysmally, so that I lost my money. Then the rotten lot split my fiver between them and drank up.

Not all the fun at shows is in the past. Just recently, after the 1983 Bath and West Show, we all gathered for a barbecue. Barbecues have become all the rage with the show jumping fraternity, and this time we had three. Harvey Smith brought his, Liz and Ted Edgar brought theirs, while Malcolm Pyrah completed the trio, and with a ring of straw bales to sit on we looked like a gypsy encampment. Most people provide their own food at these gatherings, and this evening Malcolm, Liz and Harvey cooked it. Harvey is a fantastic cook – he could be one of the best barbecue cooks in the country – and he produces some very, very delicious sauces which he puts over the steaks.

At the Bath and West our barbecue started about half-past seven to eight, and we all had plenty to eat because the girls had been to the butchers and bought steak, and we had hot potatoes and everything that goes with a barbecue. Pam provided the wine, and as there were about twenty of us we had a really good time.

Then, of course, after food and drink we were just a little bit merry and when Malcolm Pyrah suggested that we had some racing there were plenty of takers. This was not to be ordinary racing – not horse or running – but motorbike racing.

What you may not be aware of is that nowadays most riders have a light motorbike attached to their lorries. We don't use them as toys, but as a convenient way of getting from A to B. At the big shows everything is so spread out, and it is so far to go from the stables to the rings and from ring to ring, that it only becomes possible to do your job properly if you have transport of some kind. So most of us now have little Hondas that we use at Hickstead and show grounds like that to get around the rings.

At a show like Hickstead there are, as well as the main ring, several outside rings where you may be jumping your less experienced horses. You may have as many as six horses on the go in one morning or afternoon. You can have, say, two in the one ring, and another in each of two other rings, or even more. So what you sometimes do is jump one of your two horses in the first ring, hop on the bike and belt off to the next ring to ride a horse before coming back to ride the second at the first ring, and then back for a jump-off, and so on. So a bike is an essential tool of the show jumper's trade in these highly competitive times.

We had several motorbikes available that evening at the Bath and West to make a great bit of sport, and we only had one nasty spill, which involved Paddy McMahon. Now Paddy is a big lad, standing six foot one and weighing twelve stone, so you can imagine he rather overburdens a little Honda. There he was, going round our hastily improvised racing circuit with the rest of us, when it began to rain slightly. This made the grass a bit slippery, but maybe all would have been well even then had not Paddy on one bend mistaken the throttle for the brake. . . . The next moment there he was, with my bike, under a nearby Land-Rover and trailer. However, he crawled out none the worse and the bike was all right too, but by this time we'd had enough of bike racing and the inevitable water fight started.

It was rather funny really because about six of us had half buckets of water and we were all waiting there in hiding for some unsuspecting person to appear. David Bowen was the unlucky one. Out he comes, tuff-tuff-tuff, on his little motorbike, little imagining what was in store, to receive the full force of six buckets of water. Of course he was absolutely drowned, but as with all this water-fighting business he took it in good part.

Then, after the water and the wine and the barbecue and the motorbike racing, Tim Price decided that we should have some show jumping so we piled up bales of straw as fences and went jumping the horses over them with only the headcollars on. Now if anybody reading this decides to do the same, then I say please don't. What some of the most experienced riders can do with horses that are trained to a high degree of obedience is one thing; but, for many people, jumping bareback with only a headcollar is a recipe for disaster. Anyhow, our improvised bareback jumping show went on until two in the morning, as we illuminated the 'arena' with the lorry lights and I fixed up the searchlight that I always carry as an emergency lighting in case we should break down on the road. Eventually everyone decided that there was another day's jumping to come and it was time to turn in, but we certainly did have a lot of fun that evening.

So you see we make our own fun at shows, and we don't go to the pubs a lot. We nearly always stay around our caravans and when we eat in the evening we usually set up the barbecues and tuck in that way. However sometimes there is a more formal outing in the evening, such as last year at the Paris Show when we were all supposed to be going out for an evening meal with our *chef d'équipe*.

Unfortunately for me, I happened to get involved in a water

fight just after I'd changed to go out, and I was soaked to the skin. I realized that Ronnie Masserella would be round any moment and I'd have to look smart and tidy, so with that I went on the scrounge for clothes. I did manage to find a pair of my own shoes, but I had to get Paul Schockemöhle to lend me some socks. Then I went to Jeff McVean and managed to borrow some trousers, because Jeff and I are about the same size, and he also loaned me a shirt. It was a lovely warm evening, so I didn't need a vest, but there was one item missing. I didn't have any pants. I had my shoes, I had my shirt and my trousers, and I had my socks, but I had no underpants. It felt funny wearing trousers without underpants, and I hunted through our caravan high and low but couldn't lay my hands on any clean pants. So in desperation I went to one of Pam's drawers and there, of course, were several pairs of panties. So it was that I went to this *chef d'équipe*'s dinner party wearing Jeff McVean's trousers and shirt, Paul Schockemöhle's socks, my own shoes and my wife's panties. I don't know what I looked like, but the meal was good!

Without doubt one of the most action-packed and hilarious journeys we ever made was to the Austrian CSI that was held at the Stadhalle in Vienna in November. Only a little while previously we had been at Laxenburg near Vienna for the first CSIO to be held in Austria since the war, which I told you about in chapter 10. Just for the record, a CSIO is an official international meeting, and the results go forward for the President's Cup, while a CSI is an international meeting to which selected riders get invited.

For this journey we were loaned a nice big Oakley horse box which belonged to Keith Kay, one of whose horses we were riding at the time. Pam and I had our five horses with us, and the rest were going in Ted Edgar's brand new lorry, which Malcolm Pyrah was going to drive. Now Ted was very fussy about his new lorry with its coach-type chassis, and he wouldn't let Malcolm near it until he had been over to Ted's yard and had some driving lessons. This didn't go down too well with Malcolm, as it implied that he didn't know how to drive a horse box, whereas in fact he'd been driving them for years.

We left for Dover about eight in the evening to take the 3 a.m. ferry, and got to Dover with our box at around one in the morning. Malcolm is always very punctual – we'd never known him to be late. We waited and waited and then about half past two Malcolm arrived in a bit of a tizzy. He drove Ted's lorry full belt into Dover docks cursing and swearing like mad, because when he had got into it at Ted's place it wouldn't start. Luckily for Malcolm it had been Ted himself who'd got in to start the vehicle and so Malcolm couldn't be blamed. Eventually with the help of a mechanic they had got the thing going, but it had been a nerve-shattering drive down to Dover, and Malcolm was not at all happy.

It was an uneventful crossing, and we drove off at Zeebrugge to wait for Malcolm. Again we waited and waited, but there was no sign of Ted's lorry – we saw nobody and heard nothing of what was going on, and the whole boat was unloaded while we feared the worst. Eventually out of the ferry doors, bouncing alarmingly on its rather soft coach suspension, came Ted's lorry, being towed at high speed by a 'mechanical horse'. This front end of a transporter had needed the full run of the ferry floor to get enough speed to pull the big horse box up the ramp and on to the dock-side. Once more Malcolm was mouthing profanities until the air was blue. The damned lorry – Ted's wonderful new lorry – had packed up again and wouldn't start.

I suppose we waited eight or nine hours at Zeebrugge docks as they tried to fix the lorry. The papers were wrong as well, so we couldn't have gone anyway, but the delay did nothing for Malcolm's language. Eventually we got going and were *en route* for Aachen, where we were going to stable the horses and give them a rest, as it is a long long way to Austria. Malcolm knew the way – so he said – and led us successfully to the German border. We got through the border fairly easily and were fairly near to the Aachen show ground when Malcolm turned his great wide lorry down this little country lane with only enough room for a couple of thin cars to pass and with dykes both sides of it. Now I wasn't going to follow him down there because while I didn't know the way to the Aachen show ground I knew that that couldn't possibly be the way. So I waited at the top of this long straight narrow lane and suddenly we saw the stop lights come on and then more lights appear as every one in the lorry came tumbling out; Malcolm had realized that he was wrong, and that we were right – this was not the way to the show ground!

So Malcolm had to back the great lorry right the way up this lane, in great danger of sliding off into the dykes, and everyone was then treated to more of the Pyrah language and why hadn't we followed him, etc?

By the time we got to the show ground it was two in the morning, and not unnaturally they had locked up the gates of the ground and gone to bed as they had given us up. So Malcolm, who wasn't having too good a journey and wanted to get the horses bedded down and to get some sleep himself, ran straight across to the gates of the ground to try and open them. Unfortunately they were electrified to keep out intruders, and Malcolm was shot base over apex back across the concrete. Poor Malcolm, it was certainly not his trip! Locked out of Aachen, there was only one thing for it, and that was to drive on to Munich which was due to be our second resting place along the way. Judy Pyrah could drive Ted's lorry – to hell with her having no rehearsal at doing it! – and Pam would take over from me, while Malcolm and I got our heads down for the four to five hours it would take to get to Munich.

In Ted's lorry there was a drop-down bunk, as in a boat, where Malcolm went to kip, while I bedded down in the 'Luton' of our lorry. The Luton is the accommodation quarters that stretch out over the top of the cab of almost all horse transporters, whether they are big or small. Anyway, along the road to Munich, and with Pam leading the way at about sixty m.p.h., we hit some roadworks. The surface was terrible. Now because our horse box had a lorry chassis it didn't bounce, but poor Judy Pyrah in Ted's lorry with a coach chassis bounced like mad. So badly in fact that Malcolm was shot out of his top bunk and on to the floor. So, by the time we got to Munich, Malcolm was not too happy with anyone.

We got to Munich between six and seven in the morning, put the poor horses into stables and rested up so that everyone had a good day and a night's rest. Having now had some sleep we loaded the horses up at about four in the morning, intending to get to the Austrian border early as it was a difficult border post to get through. So I pulled out on to the road, but again no Malcolm appeared. This was getting a bit monotonous, and I went back to see what was wrong. There was Malcolm, laying into Ted Edgar's pride and joy with a large baulk of wood. He was being assisted by a couple of grooms, and together they were trying to close the big ramp, which just wouldn't slot in. If Ted had been able to see what Malcolm was trying to do to his lorry he would have had a fit. As it was, Malcolm was swearing at this poor unfortunate ramp. 'I'll get this f——ing ramp in if it kills me; Ted can have his f——ing lorry; I never want to see his lorry again; I wouldn't have it if Ted gave it me.'

We were a long time at the border and were so late that we decided that we must stop on the way to Vienna. Now on the Continent they have some lovely big lay-bys and we pulled into one of these to give the horses a few minutes' walk off the lorry. We had literally been walking our horses for twenty minutes or more before any of the horses from the other lorry appeared. Just then Liz Edgar's groom, who was travelling with Malcolm, came up with two horses and she was laughing all over her face. 'Why have you been so long?' we asked. 'What's happened?'

'Well,' said the girl, whose nickname was Hob. 'We've had a slight accident. Malcolm is not feeling too well. You know how we couldn't get the ramp fastened in Munich – well, when we pulled in here we couldn't get it down either. So Malcolm was standing on the tow-bar of the lorry with the handle of the ramp in both his hands pulling and pulling at it with all his might. He's pulled it so hard that it's come adrift and he's gone flying backwards across the lay-by and he's nearly knocked himself out. We've had to lay him up in the lorry to recover and we've only just managed to get the horses unloaded.'

It took poor old Malcolm a full hour and a half to recover his senses, and so when we got to Vienna we were very late indeed, and to cap it all we found that the Italians had pinched part of our stables. What they'd done was to increase the eight-foot width each horse was allowed to ten feet by moving the dividing partitions, so leaving our poor horses with widths of only six feet.

Meanwhile Malcolm was telling us exactly what he was going to say to Ted Edgar about his flaming lorry. 'You wait until I see that Ted Edgar. I'll tell him what I think of his lorry. I wouldn't have that lorry as a gift.'

Just then Ted, who had come on by air to Vienna, marched into the stables as the horses were being unloaded. 'Now then Malcolm, what do you think of my lorry? Isn't it marvellous? I bet you'd love a lorry like mine,' etc. To which Malcolm meekly replied, 'Yes Ted, I would, it's a fine lorry, I'd really love a lorry like yours.' And he sounded as if he meant it.

So after Ted had gone out of earshot we all said to Malcolm, 'We thought you were going to tell Ted exactly what you thought of his goddam lorry?'

'Well,' said Malcolm. 'I've had a horrible journey and I just couldn't face this show with Ted not liking me, could I?' As it was, he didn't have a very good show, which I suppose was not too surprising.

Very shortly another funny thing happened. Everest Milord was a very bad-tempered horse, and when the Italians refused to restore our stable space, Ted saw red. 'Right, I'll fix you, you b——s,' he muttered. 'I'll put Milord next to Ambassador.' (Ambassador was the Italians' 1972 Olympic Gold Medal horse, ridden by Graziano Mancinelli.) With that he tied Milord up with a loose rope and soon Milord was eating Ambassador; which caused such a row that the stable manager was called in. The outcome was that the Italians were ordered to put their stables back as they found them, so that all the horses had eight feet. When this was all sorted out, Ted did a characteristically wicked thing. The stable manager wore a kind of smock with big gaping pockets, and as he walked away Ted dropped his lighted cigarette into the stable manager's pocket. He was half way across the show ground before the smell of smoke made him realize that his coat was on fire. It was a bit naughty, seeing that the man had actually been responsible for sorting out our stables, but after all by then Ted, like the rest of us, was at the end of his tether!

This was not the only caper that Ted Edgar was involved in that autumn in Vienna. While we were at the show we were all invited to a traditional Viennese ball which was held at a very grand chateau. It was one of those places which you normally see only in films, where you drive up an incline to some beautiful glass doors because the ballroom is on the first floor. There the ladies and gentlemen alight and the chauffeur drives off, in much the way they must have done it in Franz Lehar's time, except that the car would then have been a coach and four.

In our case we drove up the incline to this grand entrance in a little hired car which was a paint job with the Union Flag all over it. There Ted Edgar, who was driving, decided to leave it – right smack bang by the entrance, which couldn't have made us all that popular to start with.

It was a truly Viennese ball with the men in white ties and tails and the ladies in ball gowns and white gloves. The show jumpers, who had none of these things, were ushered into a very large room adjoining the ballroom where tables were laid out – one for each team. With great hospitality each person was provided with a whole bottle of wine, and as there were some fourteen people at our table by the time we had downed fourteen bottles of wine we were all rather merry.

At this point we were joined by the British Ambassador and his wife, who were a very charming couple indeed. Half way through the meal, for some reason or other the Ambassador got up from the table and, although it was nothing to do with him, almost immediately the table collapsed. It was one of those great round tables set on a central pillar, rather like a mushroom on its stalk, and it just subsided sideways.

Seeing this disaster, the servants came in, whisked everything off and laid another table for us. They gave us all extra food and of course yet another bottle of wine. As the evening went on it got very hot and Ted decided to take his jacket off. Now apparently taking your jacket off in public is not done in Austria at all. So Ted was sitting there in his shirt sleeves, and along comes a wee little man to ask Ted if he would kindly put his jacket back on.

Well Ted, what with the drink and the heat, gave him a bit of abuse. This led to something of an argument, and a couple of us had to intervene to try to persuade him to calm down, while the little man was very disturbed indeed. There was an awful lot of very hot language passing to and fro, and as the Austrian gentleman could speak fluent English he knew exactly what Ted was saying to him. So, to cut a long story short, we were asked to depart from the ball rather earlier than we might otherwise have done.

'I hope your dance goes to hell,' said Ted as a parting shot, and out we all trooped rather the worse for wear. We piled back into our cars, including the one that proclaimed that the British would park anywhere, and off we went back to our hotel. Actually we used to get about two parking tickets a day with that car in the streets of Vienna while we were there, but no one seemed to care as the car was only on hire.

Thankfully we all tumbled into bed, and next morning woke up with very thick heads but managed eventually to go to the show as usual. So the evening came, and Ted won the main competition on Everest Milord. As we stood in line waiting to be presented with the rosettes, who of all people should come down the steps but this dear little man with whom Ted had had the stand-up row the night before! He was none other than the President of the Horse Show and I can assure you that he did not present Ted with the trophy – no, rather he thrust the thing at him and then, to emphasize his displeasure, thrust the rosette at him too. He did this in stony silence and with a grim look on his face, pointedly forgetting to shake the victor's hand in the customary way. I don't think the British got a particularly good name that trip.

This was a pity, because we were very grateful to the Austrians, who treated us extremely well and offered us lavish hospitality. For instance, the first night of the show the organizers gave a party in a hall that was next door to the stable block. There was a door between the hall and the stables where our grooms were, and we managed to get this door undone. We had absolute mountains of food and lashings of drink, and as we couldn't think of our grooms missing out we kept passing food and drink through to them, so that they could have a bit of a party as well.

This was fine until after the party, when we went down to see how our horses were faring in their new stables. In those days Jenny James was doing our horses for us, and she was a girl who normally was almost teetotal. So it was not surprising that in the British stables Jenny and some of the others were hilariously drunk and quite incapable. So we, who are rather more used to holding our liquor, had to set to and see the horses properly bedded down ourselves. It isn't something I do often – that's what I pay grooms for – but as I was responsible for their merry state it was the least I could do. It was just another memorable happening on what proved to be an absolutely unforgettable trip.

# 12 The Age of Jungle Bunny

The period following my accidents up to when I again fell on very hard times in 1984 is so tied up with Jungle Bunny that I am going to tell it through his story and add the other bits and pieces as I go along.

Spectator II, as he was then, who was going to be more successful than Freddie Welch or anyone ever dreamed of, started his career as a four-year-old in 1972, jumping the usual foxhunter classes. A foxhunter class is the first real rung up the ladder of the show jumping tree. The fences are not all that big, with the highest at four feet and only one fence at that height. In addition the horse must have won a certain amount of prize money, which today is £100. Spectator II was bred in Yorkshire and between 1972, when Susan Hutchinson bought him and changed his name to Ganderbush, and 1977, when I got him, he'd won about £900 all told. He found his way through various stables until he ended up with Freddie Welch. He was ridden by Nigel Goddard in 1976 and part of 1977, and he came to us after Pam had bought him at the Horse of the Year Show.

I told you about the first couple of months with Jungle Bunny in chapter 3, but the first big show I took him to was the Amberley Horse Show in Gloucestershire. This was at the end of March and I had, for so early in the partnership, some considerable success. I won the Scurry, won the Members' Prize, was second in the Area International Trial and was fourth and fifth respectively in two other classes. To end up winning £110 at one show after all the trouble I'd been through and on such a 'new' horse looked good for the future.

I also took Call Me Sam to Amberley; he was Pam's horse, but she was not yet riding him competitively, as she had so recently had Robert. I came back from Amberley, having done well on Jungle Bunny and also on Call Me Sam, and perhaps I prattled on too much about the good show I'd had and how happy I felt about it all. The fact was that Pam, who was probably suffering a bit from post-natal depression, didn't really share my enthusiam and would have nothing more to do with Call Me Sam after that. As far as I could see, all I'd done was to wax eloquent about her horse and say what a fantastic jumper I thought he would be. But Pam never rode that horse again.

A horse like Call Me Sam was a much easier proposition to ride than Jungle Bunny. I'll grant you that once you had him worked up he was very careful and a very clean jumper, but oh the work I had to do to get him prepared to go into a class.

Then I went to our own home ground – the Lincoln Show – and won my very first Open with Jungle Bunny. After that I took him to several more shows, winning and being placed in quite a few classes, but it was not until I went up to Morpeth, in Northumberland, and finished third in the Area International Trial that we began to build up real points for the horse as an international ride. Flushed with this success, I took Jungle Bunny on to the Bath and West and it was there that he really began to make his name. He was in the money in every class and again placed in the AIT, so that I ended up Leading Rider of the Show, which is always a coveted title and produces a great deal of joss.

From then on I took him to shows all round the country, consistently being placed – always knocking on the door and building up a reputation and the prize money. However, the first really big win for us was when he won the AIT at the South of England Show against tough opposition. We qualified for Wembley by virtue of the amount of money we had won together, but it was early days for the partnership and our best at the Horse of the Year Show in 1978 was fourth in the Sunday Times Cup. However, he was still performing consistently, being placed sixth in the Philip's Cup, eighth in the Daily Telegraph Cup, and sixth again in the Radio Rentals Cup. I was not at all unhappy about that performance as one of the most important attributes for a top-flight show jumper is consistency. It doesn't matter if he is not winning a single class. If he is staying somewhere around the same level in each class he enters, then you can improve on that, knowing what his form is at that time. If, however, you get a horse that is brilliant one minute and hopeless the next, you cannot trust him in any class. Jungle Bunny was proving consistent.

The next big show after the Horse of the Year Show is the International Show Jumping Championships at Olympia, just before Christmas, where a lot of fun is to be had and a much more relaxed and friendly atmosphere prevails than at some other shows earlier in the year. I got a second on Jungle Bunny in the Harris Carpets stakes that year, as well as several other more minor placings. However to get fourth in the Grand Prix of the show was great as far as I was concerned. My year's success on the horse was not a flash-in-the-pan, but was ending with good placings against the best competition.

At every show I entered Jungle Bunny that year he won money – except for one, Windsor, which is a show where I have in the past always done well. I was also Leading Rider at the South of England Show, where I won the Vic Boone Memorial Trophy, which is a fantastic silver trophy of a mare and foal under a tree.

Now you may remember that I said that I came back from Amberley in the spring of 1977 fully convinced that Call Me Sam would be a great jumper. That might have been so, but the partnership between me and the horse did not develop well. Maybe he was too easy a ride to be great, or maybe I need a horse that fights back – I don't know – but as it was I ended up selling him to a young rider called Suzanne Ward, from Essex, who rode him for the next two or three years with considerable success. I think, looking back on it, I felt that Call Me Sam was always almost getting there, but never quite making it for me, and so there was nothing for it but to sell him on to someone with whom he might well click. Just because you don't get on with a horse doesn't mean that no one can get on with him. His temperament may simply not fit yours, and there are innumerable cases of a great horse passing through many hands before finding a rider with whom it sparked.

In 1978 I had a horse called Wiffenpouf, which I up-graded to A status and was jumping under the Griffin and Brand ownership. She was a thoroughbred mare with which I had considerable success. There are always lesser horses than your top three going through the stables, being up-graded, so that they have made their mark and can be sold on to riders who are looking for top-grade show jumpers. Amongst these was one called Mount Falcon that belonged to a Mr Posket, who is a butcher here in Lincoln, and I jumped this horse through to Grade B standard and qualified him for the foxhunter class at Wembley. When I took him to Wembley I blew it by having a silly four faults in the final – but that's life.

In the meantime we had acquired a horse called Estelle, which was an Australian horse of some considerable ability, and Pam was riding her. At Burleigh, the Bath and West, and the South of England shows amongst others Pam jumped this horse into the money in many a class. Things were going well for the partnership until we went to the Kent County Show that year. The mare was still jumping well and Pam had her in the Area International Trial. As she turned to jump a fence the mare 'pecked' on landing, and Pam rolled over her shoulder and fell in front of the horse, so that as Estelle cantered past she trod on Pam's leg and broke it very severely in two places.

Now it was Pam's turn to be in hospital with a critical riding injury. When I arrived at the hospital in Kent, I was appalled to find that after some hours she was still in the emergency ward and no one was doing a thing about her leg. It took a great deal of anger and frustration before we found a doctor who would come along and set her leg. When we got home Pam was complaining about the leg still giving her trouble, so we went to see a bone specialist in Lincoln called Mr Smith. On examining the X-rays which he took, Mr Smith decided that they had done such a bad job in Kent that he would have to rebreak the leg and then reset it properly. In the meantime I had had a bill from the surgeon in Kent demanding payment for the work he had done. You may imagine that he got short shrift from me. In fact he got a nasty letter to which there was, inevitably, no reply – but also no further demands for money.

With her damaged leg Pam could not ride Estelle, and I was also afraid that she would get back on the horse before the bones had knitted up and we would be back to square one, so in August I put the mare on the market. I sold her to a young rider who could not have had much ability as I have never heard of the horse since. It is amazing what the rider can do for a horse. The good sympathetic rider can coax a performance out of almost any animal. In the rough, tough, world of top show jumping that horse may not hit the headlines, but will do well around the shows and earn its keep. Then you are forced to sell it on for one reason or another, and suddenly – oblivion.

Soon after I lent the horse Free Agent to Tim Grubb, and while he had him abroad the horse broke down and had to be rested. So Free Agent had to be denerved, like Tuffet, because he had damaged his foot. This was done at the beginning of 1978, and I had him back to work on. I produced him back to a state where he could jump again and took him to the August show at Morpeth, where he came second in one of the classes and got the same position in the knock-out competition. He went on to win places at many other shows and then one night the phone by the bed rang and it was Fergus Graham, a dealer I knew from Banbury. 'I want one more horse for a consignment I am sending to Switzerland,' he said. 'Would you sell me Free Agent?'

'But he's had to be denerved,' I answered.

'Doesn't matter. It will not make any difference in this case.' Now I had gone to bed early that night and it was about ten o'clock. However, we agreed a price. 'Well, my lorry is coming down the M1,' said Fergus, 'and will arrive with you about two a.m.'

So up I had to get and as I sat there in the lounge waiting, sure enough the lorry arrived, picked up the horse, and off he went to Switzerland. What they did about papers I will never know – they must have got their own paperwork done. The time interval between selling the horse and seeing the box off down the High Street was less than four hours. Yet I heard afterwards that his new Swiss owner was delighted with him and went on to win many classes with him.

During 1978 I jumped in England most of the time, although there were a couple of internationals. The first one that year was in Paris, to which I took Jungle Bunny and Ferona. After that it was Rotterdam, and again I took my first horse, Jungle Bunny, and also Wiffenpouf. I wish I'd never taken her to that show, however, because although she did not have a bad fall, and did not hit any fence very hard, somehow, somewhere during the show she cracked a bone in her leg. I didn't realize it at the time and she still did her best and jumped well for the rest of the show, but that was really the end of her jumping career as she never managed to have much success again. I went on jumping her, but she just didn't seem to have the spring she had had before. Then, in the January of 1979, while being exercised, she started to go lame; when we took her to the vet's and got her X-rayed we found that she had a fractured cannon-bone, which was irreparable, so she ended her days as a brood mare.

In 1978 Jungle Bunny had a very consistent year, but he did not actually win many classes. He did take first prize in the Everest Double Glazing Stakes in June at the South of England Show, as well as winning the Radio Rentals AIT Preliminary and coming second in the actual event; also he won the Area International Trial at Millfields in September but that was all. It just goes to show how you do not have to hit the top spot every time to be in the money, for my total winnings on him from the start of 1978 through to the end of the Horse of the Year Show, where he won the Basildon Bond Trophy, were nearly £7,000.

We clocked up that total with 13 second rosettes, 9 thirds, 9 fourths, and 33 other placings between fifth and tenth place. Jungle Bunny was a bit of a devil if you pushed him too fast round the course, and was inclined to carelessly clobber the odd fence. I was therefore unable to push on too fast in the jumps-off and there was nearly always another faster horse/rider combination to grab the top spot.

However, 1979 turned out to be Jungle Bunny's great year. In 1978 we may have been well down in the winning of major classes, but this year we came first in no fewer than eight major classes, and the true recognition came through the internationals which we attended, both official (CSIO) and by invitation (CSI).

He started to place his stamp on the year by getting a double clear round in Geneva. Then in the Paris CSIO in July he jumped another double clear round. We were picked to go to Calgary in September, Pam came too as a spectator, and I took Roscoe as second string. Roscoe made sure that he worked his passage by only having one rail down in the whole show. That single error was in the last round of the knock-out competition, and he still ended up second.

He won the very first class at Calgary and we had a super, super show, being in the money in every class. Jungle Bunny himself jumped his third double clear in the international events of that year at Calgary and my then owner, Tony Elliott, flew over to join us.

The official end of the jumping season is the last day of the Horse of the Year Show, and so when I went to Zuidlaren CSIO in December it was officially 1980 and not 1979 at all. Thus the double clear which Jungle Bunny jumped at Zuidlaren does not appear on the record books as being in 1979 yet in the calendar year 1979 Jungle Bunny jumped *four* double clear rounds in Nations Cup competitions. That is a great achievement for any horse, and I believe it is a record which has yet to be beaten by a British-bred horse ridden by a British jockey.

Also that year I was riding horses called In Gear and In Transit for the Reynolds Motor Company from Essex. I also had a horse called Puck, which belonged to François Mathy, and a mare called Tiger Tamer under the Griffin and Brand name, plus of course the usual string of novice horses that come continually through a yard like ours. Pam stuck to Roscoe as her main horse, and she had another little horse called Darina which had also come from François Mathy, but this was a mount with which not even Pam was able to do very much.

Actually we bought Roscoe that very year. We were at the Royal Windsor Horse Show when Pam saw this little rabbit of a horse jumping round with Jeff McVean on it, and she kept on to me about it until eventually I gave in and decided to buy it. So we went to see Mr Elliott and he came in half shares with us, but actually the horse had four joint owners: Tony Elliott and his wife Joyce owned one half, and Pam and I the other.

In his first year with us Roscoe won a total of nearly £900, and with this modest sum we laid the careful beginnings of a very good show jumping horse. I rode him at the Finmere Show and came second to myself on Jungle Bunny in the Finmere Championship. However, he was Pam's horse, and I only got to ride him at all because I happened to be short of a second horse on a couple of occasions, one of which was Calgary.

To tell the truth, I was a bit upset about this because, believe you me, he was the best horse I am ever likely to ride. He was only a wee little fellow, but when you sat on him you felt as if you were on a giant. He had a fantastic jump, was very brave and very careful, and as long as I live I shall never forget the few rides I had on little Roscoe. If only he had lived longer and had not had that unfortunate accident when he broke his leg, he could have been the greatest show jumper of all time.

I told you I had In Gear, whom I was running as second horse to Jungle Bunny, but she was a rather disappointing mare, always nearly getting there, but never quite making the top grade. I didn't ride In Gear for very long because I was put under pressure to drop riding for Reynolds Motors and to jump solely for Griffin and Brand. So I let Geoff Glazard have her, and he had a fantastic few seasons with her, including all but winning the Professional Championship at the Cardiff Horse Show in 1980.

Another memorable horse that year was one called LBF (La Belle Fashions); it won the Foxhunter Championship with Stuart Davidson while Pam had the ride of LBF right through 1979. We believed then that the mare had the potential to become very good, but like so many horses she never did quite get there.

However, to get back to Jungle Bunny's great year. We had gone to Gothenburg in April and been placed in some very prestigious classes which included fifth in the World Cup competition and a place in the World Cup qualifier. Then, at the Royal International, we won the Moss Bros Stakes and collected the £1,000 first prize. This was also the first Birmingham International Horse Show and I collected my biggest money win of the season simply by coming third in the Grand Prix. Then we were in the money again when we won the Everest International at the All England Jumping Competition.

So I remember 1979 very, very well because I really was at the top of the tree and my work on Jungle Bunny was paying off handsomely. However, if you imagine that all this money I am talking about went into the family coffers, you could not be more wrong.

The economics of show jumping are such that you are left with very little personal profit after all the expenses are paid, the grooms are given their wages, the entry, starting and stabling fees are attended to, the tack is renewed and the insurances are paid. After all that is deducted from the winnings, then a very usual split of what remains is 60 per cent to the rider and 40 per cent to the owner. Now when I tell you that it costs on average £2,000 to insure one horse for one year and that a very conservative estimate of the other expenses is some £5,000 a year, you will see that I have to win an awful lot of money before I can say that I have made a profit. I can truly say that if we did not buy and sell horses so that they are improved when they leave us and are therefore worth more; if we did not take paying pupils; if I did not travel the country giving lecture demonstrations, etc., I would not be able to keep my family living in the modest surroundings to which we've become accustomed.

If I remember 1979 as Jungle Bunny's year, it was because there was all the thrill of making a silk purse out of a sow's ear of a horse, and that was like drinking the summer wine. Yet 1980 was, from the outsider's point of view, an even better year because Jungle Bunny became the leading horse nationally. On the international ratings he was eighth in the world, and that is more than I could ever have hoped for him at one time.

This may sound strange, but I would always rather be on Tarzan's back than round him in the stable. Tarzan is what we call Jungle Bunny round the stables. It is a sort of curious play on ideas about the jungle, but it may also be because he is such a wild and, let's face it, vicious creature. At least he is to me. He really likes to have a go at me whenever he can, and so I have this love-hate relationship with him. Only recently I needed to go into the stable with him – and by now I ought to know better – and he got me in the corner and would not let me out. I had to call his groom, Penny, to coax him away from me because she can do anything she likes with him. Yet that is the mark of the great, intelligent horse. He is not just a dolt who doesn't know one person from another. Penny does all the nice things – I do all the nasty ones. He knows that and acts accordingly.

In the spring of the year I was joined by a horse called Jet Fresh, which Tony Elliott had bought from François Mathy, while Pam had a big bay horse called Arthur of Troy as her second horse to Roscoe. I also had another horse of François Mathy's called Puck. A horse that would have been great except that François had got a veterinary surgeon to come in one day to denerve some horses; this vet had managed to go to the wrong set of stables and had denerved the wrong ones. Unfortunately Puck was one of those who was denerved by mistake, and it made him very heavy on the forehand and very hard in the mouth. So when I got him Puck was an extremely difficult horse to ride, but even so I did have some considerable success on him, including winning the South Yorkshire Championship at the City of Doncaster Horse Show.

The jumping year started in 1980 at Birmingham, and between them Jungle Bunny and Jet Fresh gathered enough points to make me Leading Rider of the show. While I was at Birmingham Pam had gone to Bickton, near Exeter, with Roscoe and a very good young horse we had at the time called Feel Free.

In a show jumping partnership there is equal division of labour and so while Pam was competing in Exeter I had my small son Robert and his then nanny, Candy, with me in Birmingham. Now many two-year-old boys have their funny ways, but Robert was only happy when he was on the back of Pam's bay Arthur of Troy. So at the Birmingham show we kept Robert quiet and happy by sitting him in the collecting ring most of the day and half the night on this mountain of a horse. This also enabled Candy to watch the jumping, but Arthur meant more to Robert than just a sort of substitute for a grandstand seat. He took such a shine to the horse that since it returned to Sir Hugh Fraser he has hardly wanted to ride anything else. There was just one other horse which he was happy to ride, and that was the grey mare Ona Promise, which we had until recently. He used to sit up in front of his mother as she rode Ona Promise, but apart from that he has shown little inclination to ride, despite being given a pony of his own.

Amongst the wins I had on Jungle Bunny in 1980 there was

the Radio Rentals at the Royal Bath and West, which is a show I always enjoy and at which I have a lot of success; the Area International Trial at the Vauxhall Motors Show; we got £1,000 for winning the Grand Prix at the New Forest Agricultural, and just half that for winning the Championship at Finmere. The Grade A Championship at Cambridge netted another grand, but a similar win in the Horse and Hound Cup at the Horse of the Year Show only made us £650. All this difference in money winnings is because of sponsorship. If the sponsors cough up a large sum for the prizes then even quite modest shows can give big money incentives; this attracts the top names so that more people come to the show, of which jumping is only a small part. Thus the show organizers feel they are getting value for money as well, and everyone is happy.

On the other hand you can win classes at top name shows and still go away disappointed. For example in 1981 at the Horse of the Year Show I won a class and came away with the princely sum of £25 for my efforts. Yet in another class I finished up seventh and took away six times that amount. So there is no real rhyme or reason behind the money you win or the placing in which you win it, but you have to choose the events you enter carefully so as to maximize your money winnings. Owners want to realize on their investment, and if you don't manage to win enough money then they can cut up rough, as I know to my cost.

That year we went to Lucerne, where Jungle Bunny jumped a clear in one round and got a pole down in the jump-off. Then he jumped at Liège with four faults in each round. However, at the Paris CSIO we had a complete disaster at the third fence and came out with a bucketful of faults.

This was the first year that Pam took Roscoe abroad, and we were both at Paris and Liège in the team. Pam also took Roscoe to the Dublin outdoor show, whereas I took Jungle Bunny to the Dublin indoor show. While she was at Dublin Pam got invited to go to Amsterdam and Hanover, together with Liz Edgar. It was at the Amsterdam and Hanover shows that Pam first saw Wotan, who later became Ona Promise. Pam had a very successful season on Roscoe and together we pulled off the 'double' at the Royal Bath and West by becoming the leading male and female riders of the show. It is something we seem to have particularly made our own at that show in the last few years.

The consistent jumping horse is one of the most difficult things to find, and the high hopes I had for Jet Fresh, when we started off with an explosion of success at the Birmingham Horse Show, did not really come to fruition. He never quite hit top form again. Despite the fact that he won money at several shows on the Continent during the year with both Pam and me riding him, in the end we sold him back to François Mathy as he was not really careful enough to be a top-grade horse.

Pam was also doing very well on Arthur of Troy, who was owned by Sir Hugh Fraser, and she won many classes on him. He was a very consistent horse, being continually placed in the classes he entered both here and abroad. He was second string to Pam's Roscoe and he gave her a good year.

By the time 1981 arrived we were both committed to riding nothing other than Griffin and Brand horses – an arrangement which was eventually to cost us dear. At the time, however, it seemed a good idea. Tony Elliott had been very good to us and it seemed that nothing much could break the partnership we had with him.

Anyway 1981 was a bit of a hectic time for us, as Mr Elliott insisted on changing many of the horses over. I started out with Jungle Bunny and San Francisco as the first and second horses, while in reserve I had Manelito, Superbrat, a little mare called Independence, and Gondolier. Pam had Roscoe and Attorney. It was in the November of 1981 that we managed to get the ride of the grey mare called Wotan, later renamed Ona Promise.

In July I let Mike Saywell take over the ride of Lafayette, who was by then a Grade A horse. Mike found out that the horse was not really careful enough, but what then happened was that at the Horse of the Year Show I told Paul Schocke-möhle that the horse was for sale, and when he had ridden it he bought it. Funnily enough, the day after Paul had bought Lafayette, François Mathy was on the phone asking if he could buy the horse back.

In 1981 Pam took Roscoe to Rome, Liège, Rotterdam and Calgary, and at Calgary she had the remarkable distinction of being Leading Rider of the Show, Leading International Rider and Leading Lady Rider at one and the same show.

The winter of 1981 saw us exchanging three lesser horses which we had in the yard under the Griffin and Brand ownership for one from Paul Schockemöhle's yard. It was originally called Boy, but Mr Elliott immediately changed that to Boysie. At about the same time I was able to exchange a horse called Fraz, which I had bought in for a client, for a bay horse called Malt Street. Fraz had got half way through Grade C and had become careless and was knocking poles down right, left and centre. However, another client brought me in Malt Street, who had a good jump in him but was stopping. As both these horses had problems which I was able to work on I was able to do a straight swop so that both my clients had a new horse on which to try their luck.

So the 1982 season started with us having Jungle Bunny, San Francisco, Roscoe, Ona Promise, Attorney, Gondolier, Boysie and also Malt Street. There was also the novice Feel Free – a very promising mare who unfortunately later died of colic.

We started that season with a flourish. On the second night of the Birmingham Horse Show I won the main class on San Francisco, but just after I had ridden a pretty hectic round and had gone through the finish the horse slipped and I got thrown. However, as I had been through the finish and had remounted to leave the ring, I was still, of course, the winner.

Pam was Leading Lady Rider at that show with Roscoe. He really was a fantastic little animal. He only jumped in four shows in 1982 and yet he won no less than £3,470. Pam took him to both Rome and Lucerne, and at the latter he was the only British horse to jump a double clear round and so helped Britain to win the Nations Cup. Because of her prowess on Roscoe, Pam was picked to go to the World Championships in Dublin, but she took the horse to Hickstead before that to give him some experience for the World Championship. There the most awful tragedy struck because Roscoe hit a pole forward with his hind leg so that it scissored between his front legs and he broke one of them and had to be destroyed. This was terrible as he was only a young horse who was developing so consistently and was proving such a great partner for Pam. She was distraught about it, because it was just like losing a member of the family. I have never seen Pam so distressed as she was about the loss of Roscoe, and it took her months to get over the shock. As well as Pam herself, Roscoe's groom Simon was so badly hit by the tragedy that he walked round the yard for a whole week in a daze. Simon had been Tim Grubb's groom, but when Tim married Michelle and they moved to America Tim asked me if I could give Simon a job, which I did. Simon had been in sole charge of Roscoe all the time we had had him and had grown attached to the horse. So, like the rest of us, Simon grieved for the loss of little Roscoe – potentially one of the all-time greats.

There is no doubt that Roscoe was a great character; he started life as a bucking bronco rodeo horse in Australia, and then he was eventually bought by Jeff McVean after he'd been the cause of a fatal accident in the bronco ring. He was without doubt their champion bronco horse, but the law of the jungle said that poor little Roscoe was responsible for a man's death and so he had to go. Condemned as a killer, it was while he was being driven down the shoot and into a railway truck to go to the abbatoir that Roscoe jumped out over the very high side. Some say the side was six foot, others say seven, but it was certainly an immense height to jump from standing. For months he wandered semi-wild around the little Australian town where the bronco shows were held, until an aborigine boy nabbed him. This boy used to hire him out for people to have a gallop round the town. The boy used to charge a small fee for one circuit, and so long as they went on paying, Roscoe had to go on galloping. Eventually the boy sold him to another aborigine who realized that the horse possessed a big jump and so he jumped him in a few shows. As luck would have it, Jeff McVean was back visiting his own country and happened to see Roscoe. He liked him, bought him and brought him over to this country.

The first show he was taken to was the Royal Windsor and the very first time he'd walked in the ring, having only jumped a very few fences, Pam was straight there to see if the horse could be bought. With the help of Mr Elliott we bought him, and that was how we managed to acquire Roscoe – the best horse to my mind that I have ever sat on – and that includes the now almost canonized Jungle Bunny. He had the biggest 'engine' of any horse I have come across, despite not being all that big, and no fence was too massive or too high for that plucky little stray from Australia.

When we lost Roscoe the fates took a hand again. Johnny Greenwood came to me just at that time and confided that he couldn't afford to keep his horses, and he gave us the choice of buying Diamond Seeker or Fearless. That very next week, at the Bath and West, Pam tried Fearless and got on well with him. So once again we advised Tony Elliott that the horse was a good buy, and he bought him.

The very first show to which Pam took Fearless was the Lincolnshire County, and there he won a class for her. He was a good horse because, although we didn't get him until July, he won us a considerable amount in the first season. Pam also took him abroad to Liège on the Nations Cup Team, where he jumped for four faults and a clear.

So 1982 was a very mixed year for us. It started so fantastically, but then in the middle of the season came the awful tragic blow to Roscoe that clouded our whole memory of the year.

It was in 1982 also that the British Show Jumping Association ran out of money to send Nations Cup teams abroad. With the prospect that Britain would not be represented abroad I got in touch with the Spanish equestrian authorities in Madrid and got an invitation to take a team to Spain.

Having got that far I went to General Blacker and, after the usual shuttling backwards and forwards between the various committees, I got the BSJA's blessing to take a team to Madrid. I took the horses there in our lorry via the long sea crossing from Plymouth to Santander in northern Spain. That took twenty-four hours, and then I drove the eighteen-hour journey through immensely hilly and mountainous country to the Spanish capital. I had Pam's horses, my horses and Freddie Welch's horses, while Sally Mapleson, who was the fourth member, took her own box down by road as she was combining the CSIO with a tour of other shows in Spain.

The show went well for us, and it was the first time that

individuals had organized their own CSIO arrangements with another federation. Freddie Welch, being the senior rider, was appointed *chef d'équipe*, but I did most of the organizing. The Spanish authorities had originally agreed to pay the costs of transporting our horses on the boat, but when I went and told them the whole sad story of how the BSJA did not have the wherewithal at that time to finance our trip, they fell over backwards to help us financially. However, they made one condition. They would only go the whole hog if we won.

With that incentive we went out and won that Nations Cup in Madrid and so got the cost of Sally's air fares and our diesel for the lorries.

It was San Francisco's show, for out of five classes he came second in four and won the fifth. There was one bit of a disaster in that Ona Promise got cast in the box and bruised his hind leg quite badly, and we had a problem getting him sound for the Nations Cup where he jumped the two rounds with four faults and a clear. Also Freddie Welch's True Grit had broken down badly and was in considerable pain, so we had to cancel our invitation show at Barcelona and turn back for England straight away. However, we had won the Nations Cup and I produced a famous first by organizing the only 'private' British team to ever have been seen at a CSIO.

I took Jungle Bunny and San Francisco to several official and invitation international meetings in 1982, but I missed the first day of the Rotterdam because, while I had been schooling the horse through my own Devil's Dyke at home, the horse turned over and knocked me out. Now I don't know quite how this accident happened, but what I do know is that I spent all day in bed. I rather anticipated missing the whole show, but somehow I rallied myself and started a day late with the threat hanging over me that unless I jumped a class that day I would not be able to qualify for the Grand Prix. I remember saying to Ronnie Masserella when he told me this: 'Don't worry Ronnie, the old boy [meaning Jungle Bunny] won't let me down.' And, sure enough, in the qualifier we came second to Paul Schocke-möhle's legendary Deister.

San Francisco was good, but he still did not outdo Jungle Bunny, because the old war-horse was on the Nations Cup teams at Aachen, Paris, Liège, Rotterdam and Hickstead, and at Rotterdam we were second in the Grand Prix with our biggest single win of the season of nearly £1,500. Then in November there were the two German CSIs at Hanover and Berlin, and again in Hanover we collected a big purse for another second place in the Grand Prix. Between these two shows Jungle Bunny won nearly £3,000, which was a good way to end up a rather mixed year.

There is a story behind how we got Boysie. It was after the Paris show that the German team's lorry was involved in a bad accident and one horse was killed while the famous Deister looked like losing an eye. It was to guard against that eventuality that Paul Schockemöhle bought Boy, but when Deister came through and was certain to be OK, Paul rang Mr Elliott and offered him the horse that was to become Boysie. As I have already told you, the deal involved several of our other horses, but the horse was brought to Hickstead for the August meeting and he and I clicked immediately, so that the next day I came second in a class having never been on him until the day before. It was an instant partnership, and we came good together much more rapidly than Paul had expected, because when I had gone over to see him before we bought the animal, Paul had said, 'Take it easy on him. Give him a year's gentle schooling and you will then have yourself a great horse.' As it was, it didn't take a year or a month or even a week for me to realize that here was my kind of horse. We still went gently on Boysie that autumn and winter, although I did take him to Hanover and Berlin. His showing at Hanover over a massive course was not marvellous, but in Berlin he was much more successful.

Coming almost up to date with the 1983 season, Pam had Fearless as her number one horse, though Ona Promise was being ridden jointly because both were very good horses and she used them alternately for the big classes. I had Boysie, Jungle Bunny, San Francisco and Gondolier, and by this time I had made up my mind that my horse for the future was to be Boysie, as Jungle Bunny was now getting towards the end of his jumping career. Number two was San Francisco, with J.B. third and Gondolier fourth, and that is how I jumped them throughout the 1983 season.

Like all seasons 1983 had its ups and downs but in show jumping if you learn to live with the downs the ups come really easy.

Anyway this year we agreed with Mr Elliott that we would not do as much travelling abroad as we had done the previous year and would jump a lot more in England. However, Pam was picked to go to Dublin and to Rotterdam, where I joined her on the British team. In his very first Nations Cup in Rotterdam Boysie pulled out all the stops and jumped a double clear.

Pam had a wonderful season on Fearless, and again we shared the Leading Gentleman and Leading Lady Rider spot at the Bath and West, and at other shows too she did very, very well. However, Fearless was not a good horse indoors. He didn't seem to like the claustrophobic conditions, and as it is the indoor shows where television coverage is most valuable to owners like Griffin and Brand, we found ourselves under pressure from Mr Elliott to do more than well at these shows. Pam did a marvellous job in winning over £2,000 on Fearless at the Royal International, but it was not good enough, and it was not long before negotiations were concluded with the Italians to sell him to them for their team. We obviously did not want to lose so promising a horse, but as time went on the pressure on us built up and we eventually saw him go to Raymondo D'Inzeo during the Olympia Show, with the 1984 Olympic Games in mind.

On the other hand Ona Promise was a very good horse indoors, and with Pam riding him he ended up winning some £8,000. At the end of the season I was short of a horse and so I jumped him at Olympia, where we did well, finishing third in the World Cup Qualifier amongst other placings. At the Towerlands (Essex) Show I was second on him in the Championship and so for both Pam and me Ona Promise did well and showed great promise for the future – a future however that was not to be.

There were certain cracks appearing in our relationship with Mr Elliott in 1983. For one thing, we went to Salzburg and Luxembourg in September and did well, but not well enough.

Pam won a big class in Salzburg, and together we managed to win the Pairs event with her on Ona Promise and me on Jungle Bunny in Luxembourg. However, our expenses were so high that what we were winning was not enough to cover the cost of the trip.

This was the year when the Royal International was held outdoors for the first time in recent years. My young memories of the White City were of not doing as well there on my ponies as I had come to expect, but I did have a great show at the White City in 1983. It was a real treat for me to be riding outdoors in that very nostalgic arena, and all our horses went well there. That included Boysie getting second to Eddie Macken in the puissance event. However, there was another great win at the White City that really pleased both Pam and me. In the Bowers-Welcome Groom's Stakes, where they gave awards to the Grooms of the Year, my girl Penny won it and Pam's girl Tina shared second place with several other grooms.

I have told you how, when I got Boy from Paul Schocke-möhle, he had from the depths of his great experience told me to spend the winter schooling him, warning me that if I didn't over-face him or ever hit him, I would have a top Grand Prix horse. So I did just that, and did all I could to encourage him and tell him what a good boy he was, and he rewarded me very well. In that first and only season I had on him he won over £11,000, and he had that consistency that is so important in the horses on which you have to earn your money. In 1983 there were only four shows where he was not in the high-ranking prize money, and in 1984 he would undoubtedly have doubled his winnings, so it was the greatest wrench to lose him.

To have brought a horse on slowly and to have still won so much money in one season without ever having really pushed him showed that Paul's faith in me as one of the few riders in the world who could have brought that horse to the top of the tree was justified. It remains to be seen if anyone else can achieve that potential or if, as so often happens when a partnership is broken, the horse disappears into oblivion.

There are many reasons for exchanging mounts, but in the case of Gondolier, although he was small by show jumping standards, he was also very strong. I just knew that I was not getting the best out of him, so I exchanged him with Paul for a horse called Famos. In his turn Paul sold Gondolier to Thomas Freumann, who is perhaps the strongest rider in the world today. Since Thomas got him the steering problems which I had with him have disappeared, and he is winning some really top classes.

However, Famos was not a horse suitable for the English courses, where the poles are light and fall easily. On the Continent they build the fences with much more massive poles which the horses can rap quite hard without them falling. So many Continental horses go through life hitting the poles as a matter of course, but when they get over here they go on clobbering them and knocking them down.

So we sent the horse back to Paul Schockemöhle and we again exchanged him for a super novice horse called Pinto. Pinto was a chestnut horse, making about 16.1 hands, who had been turned out in a German field for two years and was now a seven-year-old. When we got the papers through we found he was already Grade B and while I only had time to take him to a few shows he was showing great potential.

We decided to make it slightly evident what we thought of the sale of Fearless by calling the replacement horse Pavarotti. Luciano Pavarotti is the Italian opera tenor who, having rung up Paul Schockemöhle to see if the horse was as good as he had heard it was, must have been at least partially responsible for the Italians putting up the money to buy Fearless for the Olympics. It was, we thought, a rather appropriate gesture.

Amongst the last acquisitions of 1983 was the chestnut Hawk which Mr Elliott had seen jumping at Paul's yard when he was over there. He liked the horse and managed to buy him at the Schockemöhles' autumn sale. He proved in the short time we had to be a very careful, clean jumper, and we took him to Zuidlaren with us in early December where Pam and he were narrowly beaten into second place in the mini-Grand Prix. With this promise we brought Hawk on slowly through the winter of 1983/84 with a view to putting him into our string in 1984.

As is our way all the horses were given a good rest, right through into March, which was possible this year because the very early Birmingham Horse Show, which usually comes at the end of March, was cancelled, and we decided with our owner to allow the horses to have more rest than usual, some fourteen weeks. I rarely turn my horses out in the winter because it is bad to cosset your important horses right through the season and then think it is going to be good for them to be turned out for a 'rest'. Horses today are living just as unnaturally as humans and need to be kept in sheltered, dry conditions during their rest period. They still need exercise, which we do on a patent rotary walker that I manufactured through my own company. Of course they get good food and end the winter fat and contented, which is the way it should be when you are going to expect them to give a 100 per cent effort for the other nine months of the year.

When I started to write this book I didn't know how I was going to end it. It seemed it would be a continuing story of changing horses and changing fortunes – the usual constant relatively minor ups and downs that go with a show jumping yard. I didn't know then, but I do now. When I had my bad accidents there were times when I was sure we were finished, and when Pam had her bad fall in 1978 she thought for a while that she was finished too. Yet we struggled through those times. I thought that fate could not have any more devastating blows to deal us, but there I was wrong. I was about to suffer perhaps the biggest blow I have ever received.

# 13 Friday the Thirteenth

Professional show jumpers cannot survive unless someone somewhere is prepared to put up money to keep them jumping. The owner or sponsor is therefore a necessity, but it is rather like working for someone without any terms of employment, written or unwritten, to ensure that you get treated fairly. The owner can withdraw his or her support at a moment's notice and there is not a blind thing you can do about it.

Even with a generous owner, who feels he is getting a return on his investment when you do well and get the name of his company in the headlines, there is still not much left at the end of the day for you and your family. So in 1976 I started to supplement my money by doing 'clinics'. I set up my own one-night-stand lecture demonstrations, which have been pretty successful over the eight years that I have been doing them.

During those same eight years we were building up our association with Tony Elliott. During that time we 'educated' him in the art of choosing show jumpers for us to ride, so that in the end we were quite happy to let him go and choose a horse for us, knowing that it would be the kind of animal which had a good chance of making something. We built up a partnership with him that many a show jumping set-up would envy and we became such good friends that we had no compunction in having the whole of our yard under the Griffin and Brand (European) name.

Despite what has happened since, it would be churlish of me not to acknowledge that the great revival in our fortunes following my accident, and again during the time after Pam broke her leg, would not have been possible without an owner like Tony Elliott. To get to the top and stay there you have to have the wherewithal to spend tens of thousands of pounds on the animals which the top riders are always looking for. It is a funny game, show jumping, for in no other top sport would so much be spent to recoup so little but fame and prestige. Snooker players, who only have to chalk a cue, walk away with top prizes of £20,000 to £30,000. Golfers do even better, and their expenses, compared to ours, are peanuts. Race-horse owners have the chance of making really big money if they hit a winner and the trainers who are any good at all are bound to find enough winners in a season to keep themselves going despite the number of horses they have. Meanwhile the Betting Levy Board keeps a constant supply of cash feeding into the horse racing industry. The training stables have to compete for it, but it is there. Show jumping has to rely entirely on the generosity of sponsors and owners, and with the great names of the last twenty years now fading somewhat with age, and the constant increase in the height of the money-winnings hurdle that has to be scaled (if riders are to compete at the top prestige shows like the Horse of the Year Show and Olympia), the potential sponsors see less and less likelihood of a return on their investment. So fewer and fewer riders will be able to find the cash to compete at the top, because they will not be able to win the big money if they are debarred from the top shows where they *could* win that big money.

So, with the top-of-the-tree show jumping getting more and more difficult and costly, I can see myself in the years ahead developing even more the training side of my business. I spend a great deal of time training riders who come to me – or to whom I go – as well as travelling all over the world training horses and their riders.

I have in my time trained young riders who have since become household names. The first rider whom I had any real success with was a lad called Michael Jay. He won the National Young Riders Championship at Hickstead. Then there was Pip Nichols, who won the National Young Riders Championship and the National BSJA Championship in the same year. My third highly successful boy was Tim Grubb, whose name is of course now known all over the world. He married Michelle Macavoy, now lives full time in the States, and was one of our own Olympic protagonists in 1984. These have been the most successful of my male pupils, but more recently Jim Edgeson won a Vauxhall car by being the Vauxhall Young Rider of the

Year. He won that at Olympia on Malt Street. Unfortunately Jim had some problems at home. I let him take some horses of mine, but this did not work out at all well and now I honestly don't know what he is doing. Jim is, to my mind, a boy with immense talent, but unfortunately one of the many potentially great riders who lack the money to keep them in the mainstream of jumping and so become lost to the sport just when they could be making the grade.

Amongst the girls I have trained I can pick out Vicky Gascoigne, Jean Germany and Jane Smith, who was the Leading Rider in Juniors for several years. There was also Debbie Safell, who is one of our leading event riders. When she had had a year's training with me she won the Leading Junior Show Jumper of the Year in 1974 at Wembley on a pony called Rockwood Cedric, with Vicky second on Telstar. The best-known name amongst these girls at present is of course Jean Germany, who has been winning top classes since 1977 when she was in the British junior team that won the gold medal in Switzerland. In 1978 she missed the individual gold medal in the European Championships by just 1.6 seconds. At the age of twenty she turned professional and has been sponsored until recently by Crown Paints and now DAF. Jean's list of top victories includes the Daily Mail Cup and the Radio Rentals Champion Horseman at the same 1980 Royal International. She has been in the World Cup final at Gothenburg and won many other good classes.

It is pleasing to train young riders and see them go on to win events which you wouldn't mind winning yourself, but I must say that for fun and enjoyment – plus some pretty hard work – I need my clinics. These have taken me to every part of the UK and recently to Ireland. This is to be a regular twice-a-year event, so as to introduce the young riders over there to the new ideas which a fresh face can provide.

Amongst the foreign countries where I have run clinics are Saudi Arabia, the Sudan, South Africa, Zimbabwe and Italy. Both Pam and I are eagerly awaiting the day when they feel the need for show jumping clinics in Japan, as that is a country both of us would very much like to add to our list.

With experience I now restrict the clinics to a maximum of

two days, because owing to the intensity of the training both horses and riders get very tired and cannot cope properly with three days. Then in the evenings I do lecture demonstrations, which I try to treat in a professional but light-hearted manner so that people not only get instruction and information but also have fun. I get a great deal of enjoyment out of taking new horses brought in by riders who want to improve, and riding them with all their faults. That means that mistakes occur and everyone sees that perhaps there is a chance for them as well if Lionel Dunning has had a pole down or a refusal or something with their own horse. Then you have to assess rapidly what the horse can be expected to achieve in the future; in many cases it is likely to get no further than foxhunter-type classes, as it is not a sharp enough animal.

There have been (and will be yet) some tales of woe told in this book, but let me say on the other side of the coin that show jumping has been good to me. It has taken me to places abroad to which once upon a time I would never have imagined going. I have met and mingled with many famous names in the show jumping world, and on the whole I have found them to be a hard-riding, hard-swearing, but straight and honest bunch of people. They have been the kind of people I get on with and can relate to, because they have no 'side' about them. They earn their money dangerously and with a great deal of sweat and toil, and they learn to live with intense disappointments as well as immense elations. I am in some ways glad that money has not, even now, come to blight the face of show jumping, which is still the cleanest, most open sport in the world. That has been its greatest draw with the public, because you either hit a pole or you don't; the horse either refuses or it doesn't. If you fall off, then they can see exactly what has happened and know what the penalties are. It is also a sport where the old individual qualities of courage and good sportsmanship prevail. You have beautiful and powerful animals, ridden with great care and precision by men and women of an ability which only those who try to ride horses over fences in the show ring can hope to appreciate. For every one who makes the top a thousand fall by the wayside, but they have become better people for having to think not only of their own personal ambitions, but also of the flesh-and-blood animal that enables them to do it at all. You cannot weep over breaking a snooker cue, nor over a bent golf club, but you can and do weep bitterly for the horse you love that breaks a leg and has to be put down.

Nevertheless, you have to realize that to me a horse is a tool of my trade. You may own a horse and love it, and keep it with great personal sacrifice until its dying day. I cannot be so sentimental. I hope you will understand when I say that Jungle Bunny, whom I love-hate more than any other horse I have ever had, is coming near to the end of his jumping life.

Ever since I've had him he has been treated like a god. He has the best food, the best stable in the yard, the best position when travelling. Nothing has been too good for that horse over the years. Soon I may well have to take the cold-blooded decision to have that horse put down after he retires. This is to me pure realism. To turn him out in a field would be for him a living death. To keep him in a stable and only occasionally hack him out would be something he would no longer understand. Where were the big fences and the flow of adrenaline? Where were the shouts of the crowd and the excitement of travelling to somewhere new each week to compete? As I think about it now – and thankfully it has not come to that yet – 'Tarzan' will have to submit to the law of the jungle when his time comes. However, as my wife considers that I am rather callous over things like this, it may be that I shall in the end have to compromise, but whether Jungle Bunny will be happier alive than dead I have my doubts.

Having never been turned out for years, the day he retires he is going to have to be kept in a stable and looked after. He is bound to be bored to tears with inactivity, and then of course arthritis is pretty certain to set in, so that he ends up crippled. Is that the way to treat your best friend?

The year 1984 started happily enough. We had decided we wouldn't be able to afford a holiday when quite out of the blue Raymond Brooks-Ward rang me and asked if I would like to go to Egypt. Now Egypt is one country that Pam has always wanted to visit. Ever since we've been married she has been on to me to get myself a training job in Egypt so that she could come too. Now I have been training in Saudi Arabia, where she

Jumping with Fanny Hill at La Baule, in France, where I was pushed into second place every night by the late Hartwig Steenken. Fanny was a great horse, but just couldn't beat Hartwig's Cosmos and Simona for first place. Fanny died peacefully in the field only a few months ago, having previously borne me two foals.

The victorious Nations Cup team at Calgary in 1982, with the British *chef d'équipe* Ronnie Massarella standing proudly in front. Left to right: me on Jungle Bunny, Tim Grubb on Night Murmur, Malcolm Pyrah on Law Court, and the late Caroline Bradley on Marius.

Two heads are better than one. Pam and I are looking at a course plan – and not much liking what we see.

Although in the ring we are all out to win, off duty we are a very tight-knit bunch. Here David Broome, Harvey Smith, Graham Fletcher and I are taking a long, hard look at a course at Hickstead – and again we don't seem very enthusiastic.

If you ask a horse to do more than he feels he can, then things go wrong.
Here, at the 1983 Birmingham Horse Show, Jungle Bunny just hasn't made
the height and we are both heading for a fall. In the past I never jumped J.B.
in puissance events, because you don't do that with your best horse. Anyway,
the old boy could always do seven feet, but ask him to do more and he
wouldn't make it.
This time all we had to do to get second prize was to reach the far side of the
fence – and this is how we did it.

Jumping with Jungle Bunny back in the late seventies, using a breastplate to ensure that the saddle stays put and thus keeps the rider's weight more or less over the centre of gravity of the horse. In those days I rode J.B. in a gag-snaffle, but now I ride him in an ordinary pelham.

I get a lot of pleasure from teaching young riders the tricks of the trade. These are two of my pupils, riding a couple of potentially great show jumping horses, Gomez and Gonzales, both of whom came originally from Paul Schockemöhle. After being sold back to Germany they have now returned to this country and are jumping with considerable success.

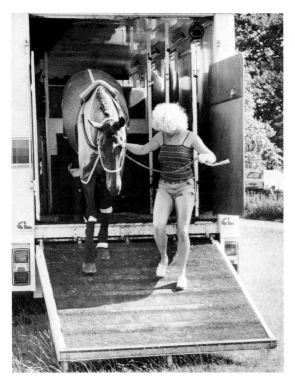

It needn't always be jods and jeans for the grooms, especially when it gets as hot as it was at Chatsworth in 1983. Here my groom Penny Morrell leads out Fearless. At the White City Horse Show the stipendiary steward asked her to cover up a bit – but he also asked for her telephone number!

Legs are the most important part of a jumping horse and need care and skilled attention. Jungle Bunny has just come into the yard from work, and another groom, Barbara, is hosing him down. Knowing what he thinks of me, I am keeping a safe distance.

The camel races were always a favourite with the Olympia crowd. Here I am being 'assisted' into the hump by the Ted Edgar broom, while Malcolm Pyrah looks on, Nick Skelton gives me a push with the end of the ladder, and Tony Newbery makes sure the beast doesn't turn round and bite me.

Dogs are an important part of our household, together with the odd lamb from our flock of sheep and our raucous grey parrot. The Jack Russell is called Katie, after our Nanny in the past. Despite the animals – and the humans – Pam always manages to keep the lounge looking immaculate.

Boysie at his best. With more experience he will be a jumping machine to rank with great horses like Eddie Macken's Boomerang.

Conversation piece at Chatsworth Park, including (clockwise) Pam, Geoff Glazard, Stephen Hadley (with the hat), Robert Smith and me. On the blackboard is Mr Tomlinson, who runs the Yorkshire show circuit and is a great friend of show jumping, while Jungle Bunny seems to be trying to pick up some tips.

came with me, and to many other countries, but Pam was keen to look round the pyramids because she is very interested in Egyptology and everything that goes with it.

The tour was the brainchild of Sammy Mahmoud, who is the owner of Michael Whitaker's Disney Way. Raymond Brooks-Ward did all the organizing this end for the three shows that were to be held in Cairo. We were there for twelve days, starting on 1 February, and the whole thing was extremely well run. The team included Harvey, whom we met there. He and his wife Irene had been on a tour of Africa and they came back to Cairo. There was John Whitaker and his wife Clair, and Michael with his wife Veronique (although she didn't ride), plus Malcolm Pyrah and Judy and Nick Skelton and Sarah; on the same plane there was also Eddie Macken and his wife Suzanne, Paul Darrah and his wife, and James Kernan who eventually teamed up with Kate, our nanny – we were able to take Kate and Robert with us – and Kate and James made up the party with no odd ones out.

Now Sammy Mahmoud had, at the Cairo end, organized a really great show which was held in three different arenas. The first of these was at a private club; the second show next day was at the Police Academy; and the third show was held at the hotel where we were staying. The Hotel Concorde certainly measured up to any of the places I have ever stayed in – and I have been all over the world. It was also a fantastic show in that, despite the length of time all we riders were together, there were never any arguments. From the time we left England to when we arrived back a fortnight later I don't think I ever heard a cross word uttered about anything or anybody.

After the show was over Sammy arranged for us to go down the Nile; that was a trip that took three days and took us down as far as the Aswan Dam where we were able to see the ruins of Abu Simbel, the temple complex which they removed to higher ground before the waters rose. Then we flew back from there to Cairo and spent the last day at Giza touring the pyramids, which was absolutely fantastic. We packed a tremendous lot into that last day, not only 'doing' the pyramids in a very thorough fashion, but also visiting an island in the Nile which was stocked with tropical plants and trees, many of which I recognized because they had been brought from the Sudan where I had been training in previous years. Raymond Brooks-Ward was with us, and being a sailing man he hired a boat and took some of the lads for a sail on the Nile, which they all thoroughly enjoyed. The last evening in Cairo was spent on a boat which plied up and down the river as we sat and ate a really marvellous meal. At the end of the evening they treated us to an authentic belly-dancer, and by the time she'd finished she had all of the show jumping males on the floor trying to gyrate their bellies in the way she was doing – and most were not succeeding, I can tell you. All that is except for Michael Whitaker, who was absolutely marvellous at going through the contortions and really kept our end up with the locals.

Our departure from Cairo by coach next day was not without incident, because when we got to the airport the travel agent had not arrived with our tickets or passports and it took Raymond a full hour to get the matter cleared up. It turned out in the end that the travel agent had taken the passports and tickets straight to the customs, but hadn't told anyone. As we were such a big party the plane couldn't go until we boarded, and so it also took off an hour late.

That Egyptian tour looked like being the start of another great season for the Dunning family, but it was not to be. During February Mr Elliott had approached me and said that he wanted Ona Promise to be reserved for the Olympic Games. We agreed to this, and we took the horse to Stoneleigh for Michael Whitaker to try, but he didn't get on too well with the horse and so after lunch, when he had had a couple of hours' rest, Leslie McNaught was put on him and Ona Promise went absolutely fantastically for her. It was 16 March that Leslie tried out Ona Promise and we agreed to keep the horse fit and well, but I couldn't take him to the Towerlands Show that came up just then because Mr Elliott did not want the horse jumped indoors but only outdoors. We then took the Griffin and Brand horses to the Lincolnshire and South Humberside Show on 31 March and 1 April.

After that we spent three days making a training video, which was sponsored by Ken Boyfield from Coventry, and I had arranged to go to have a meeting to discuss the 1984 season with Tony Elliott on Sunday 8 April at 2 p.m. In the meantime, on 5 April, Ronnie Massarella had come to my house for the evening and we'd discussed taking Ona Promise to Spain for Leslie, so that she could get used to him in a foreign arena; she would have him fit and well for competing in the Olympic Games. I believed that she could ride him well. He has all the scope, all the ability and indeed all the makings of an Olympic horse.

After the meeting with Ronnie I telephoned Tony and we spoke about having this meeting on 8 April to discuss the 1984 season in full. Well, little did I realize it, but this was to be the day that was to completely change my life yet again. I arrived at the Elliotts' house and Mrs Elliott made us the usual cup of tea. It was as I sat down, ready to discuss the riding we would do for him and his company in the coming season, that Elliott dropped the bombshell. He told me right out of the blue that he had arranged with another rider to ride for him and that therefore I would be losing all my horses.

It was without doubt the most terrible shock I have ever had in my whole life. Being told that you wouldn't ride again because your arm was useless was nothing compared to this. I had been visiting this house and this man for eight years and we'd always got on well together. Tony Elliott had been good to us in many ways, and we had been happy to put all our eggs in his basket. There seemed no reason why we should not, but I have never felt so awful as I did that afternoon when I realized that he meant what he said and that we were finished as a yard.

It was not a question of *perhaps* you will lose your horses – it was more than that. We'd already lost all the horses, because he had made secret approaches to another rider to ride for him – and he refused to tell me who this other rider was. I frantically cast about in my mind for ways of softening this blow. Could I keep some of them and try to find another owner or a sponsor, but no – it was all settled. I was bluntly told that the decision had been made to take the horses from my yard, and that was it.

So, after eight seasons and having got myself into the position where I was riding for one company, and one company only, that company just upped and pulled the rug out from under my feet and we were left with nothing. No horses on which we'd spent so much time and trouble, and no owner to buy any more. We were sunk!

The horses, I was told, would be picked up on the following Monday because that would be the most suitable day for all those concerned – other than me. Then on Thursday the phone went again – the plans had been brought forward – the yard would be cleared the very next day. So it was that on Friday the thirteenth of April – the somewhat superstitious me repeats this, Friday the thirteenth – those eight years of planning and eight years' work were thrown to the four winds. Mr Elliott arrived with two drivers and, without even telling me where the horses were going had the Griffin and Brand horses loaded up and taken away. There was just one horse left in the yard, and if that one had gone I don't know quite what I would have done. Jungle Bunny, being jointly owned by them and us, was left to thrust his dark head with its little white star over the stable door to wonder where all the other horses could have gone to. In that he was thinking the same as we were.

It was awful to look out of the back door at a ghost yard. Previously there were all these contented faces poking out over stable doors, expectantly waiting to see what was laid on for the day – and now there was nothing.

I was so shattered that I lay awake all that Friday night thinking about the horses and what we'd done with them – turning over in my mind what kind of mistakes I had made – what I might have done to upset the Elliotts that they had treated me in this way – and too stunned for deep anger. The successes, the failures, the triumphs and the disappointments ran through my tortured mind that night. I hoped it might be just a nightmare, but when I walked out into the silent yard that Saturday morning, there I was back in 1976 at the trough of our troubles. Suddenly a sharp flash of remembrance burst across the scene. I was getting out of the car after Pam had brought me back from Balham hospital and walking down the empty yard. Then, with my mind cloudy I hadn't registered it consciously, yet I must have drunk it in because there it was springing freshly to mind as if it were yesterday. I knew, as I walked slowly through the sad yard to the end box which is Jungle Bunny's, that I was feeling the self-same way as I had done then. It was a deep, deep feeling of loneliness – of being abandoned by whatever gods look after me. I turned to walk back, and Robert came running out into the yard – 'Daddy, Daddy, it's breakfast-time!'

Suddenly I realized it was not 1976. There was my kid who needed me, there was Pam indoors cooking breakfast who needed me, and there were grooms and a nanny who needed to keep their jobs. Immediately I thought, to hell with them all! Come on man, pull your socks up! You've done it before and you can do it again! How and where we are going to go, I don't know, but by God they are not going to finish us.

I still didn't know where or how it would be done, but I began making plans – lots of plans – and from that moment I started to turn my anger at the disgusting way I had been treated into action, so that the yard would soon be full of horses again. What they would make – what we would make of them – I had no idea, but the dead lucky Dunnings, Lionel and Pam, were on the way up again.

# 14 A Fresh Start

At one time I thought I might have to end this story with the coincidence of chapter 13 and the horror of Friday the thirteenth, but so much has happened since then that I want to tell you about it.

After the horses had gone it really did hit me, and I walked about for a week or even more in a sort of trance. More than that, I had lost confidence in myself. I felt vulnerable. It was a vast shock to find how quickly you could go from being one of the top-flight show jumpers to nothing. Yet I knew that I had to start again somehow when the will to do it returned.

As I wandered about, thinking up first this idea and then that idea, I gradually began to see some light. The first thing I did was to advertise in the equestrian press for horses. Very much to my surprise – and also to my delight – several of the owners I had had before the Griffin and Brand period contacted me. Despite the fact that I perhaps had not spoken to them for six or seven years, they still wanted to have their horses with me, and that was a great boost to my morale. By the end of the fortnight after the Griffin and Brand horses had gone, my yard was teeming with horse life again.

Now this was a step in the right direction, but it was not what I was eventually aiming at. I would have liked to have top-grade Grand Prix horses, but these lesser creatures that poked heads out of stables all over the yard were bread and butter – and at least I was feeding my family. People were also asking me to break horses for them, and I was refusing nothing that might make some money and keep the wolf from the door. So I began to feel a bit like Paul Schockemöhle who, when he has been out and bought a load of horses, thinks nothing of putting them three or four to a box. Now over here the thought of several horses in one box is shocking, but in Germany it is done all the time. I never had to have more than two to a box, and in any case it was only temporary as the tide of people swept to my door.

From this beginning I began to acquire Grade A horses, and I brought dear old Jungle Bunny back into work, even if I was at first only jumping him in small classes. I was asked by Mrs Redbart to take on Synapse, a horse that her daughter had found rather difficult. I also got Dicey's Scholar from Philip Lanni, the brother of John Lanni who is *chef d'équipe* to the British Junior Show Jumping Team. Their other brother Carmen is a great trainer of horses and he actually trained Jungle Bunny as a four-year-old. He also trained Debby Johnsey's famous horse Speculator and many others.

However, horses like Dicey's Scholar were simply birds of passage and really my yard was full of young horses waiting to be broken, young horses that had yet to get to a show, or Grade A horses that nobody else wanted. These latter horses were ones which had perhaps not been jumping for a couple of years and so represented a great deal of potential work. So while I had quantity there was very little quality, and if I was to get back into the international show jumping scene I was going to have to acquire some top horses of the same calibre as Jungle Bunny, Boysie and San Francisco.

So 1984 has seen a complete change in my life-style. People know I am home, and the phone never stops ringing with requests for me to do training. Every week there are two or three people here with their horses being trained or waiting to be trained. So now I go on the road only two days a week rather than the five days as I did before.

However that doesn't mean that I have not had a successful year of show jumping. For example Jungle Bunny, despite being in his twenty-first year, won his qualifying money for Wembley very easily. He has been backed up by Synapse, who incidentally is a little French chestnut that was once one of the best horses in France and was then purchased by Mrs Redbart for her daughter a few years ago, but has never hit the headlines since then. Unfortunately he has a bit of a dirty stop in him. He doesn't refuse like a normal horse: he waits till he's two feet off the floor and then decides to put his feet down again, and that has resulted in two broken ribs and one cracked one – all mine!

But I have him because he is difficult and he *is* a class horse.

As well as Synapse I have had Bobtail, who belongs to Mr Malcolm Clarke, of Clarke Steels from Manchester; and Pam has had a super mare, Brickhall Terri, from him also. She has brought the mare on from a novice until now it is within an ace of being Grade A and has also qualified to jump in the Godfrey Davis final at Wembley. I still have Mr Bonsal's Maltstreet, and for a while Ted Edgar loaned the Countess of Inchcape's Whato.

At the Royal Show they built a course that was to give the amateurs a feel of what they would face in Los Angeles in the Olympic Games. When we walked the course it was not just huge, it was enormous, and in the event the first three places were all taken by professionals. I led the field, with a quarter of a time fault, until near the end of the class when Malcolm Pyrah managed to jump the only clear round of the competition, and so I had to be content with second place.

I decided soon after the loss of my Griffin and Brand horses that the way back was not to attempt to rival the top notchers with their Grand Prix mounts, but to become a big fish in a much smaller pool. So I have built up my confidence again at lesser shows, and have still managed to win the money through using Jungle Bunny as my first horse and Synapse etc. as second string. For instance, Jungle Bunny won close on £1,000 at the Kent County Show and Synapse was second in another high-yield class at that show. At the Hillingdon Show in Middlesex I did so well with these two horses that I was leading rider. While I was at Hillingdon I was asked to ride another good horse called Spirit of Lee, and he has proved to be a horse I can get on with. I was fourth in the 'Derby' in Copenhagen on him and he has won me several good classes at shows in this country.

This trip to Denmark was the first rung back on the international ladder, but it was an invitation show for which all expenses were paid by the Danes. I went over with Mike Saywell, and between us we managed to get placed better than fifth in every class in the show.

Back here at Birmingham Jungle Bunny really hit form. I won the AIT on him and the Show Championship into the bargain. I was second in the Topscore, and Synapse won a class and was placed second in two other classes. In addition, Spirit of Lee was third in the Two Fence Challenge, which most riders will know as an upmarket Chase-me-Charlie.

So all in all the softly, softly, catchee monkey approach I have adopted all through this long hot summer of 1984 has been paying off. So much so that I have been again recognized as an international rider fit to be included in the British team, and as I write this I am off to Lisbon in a few days' time to join Graham Fletcher, Michael Mac, Gary Gillespie and the Scottish rider Janet Hunter to represent my country abroad once again. That is something which only a few short months ago I could not see happening for a very long time – if at all. I was floored and I couldn't then see how to get up, let alone continue the fight and win, but gradually things have been panning out. Windfalls like the potential Grand Prix horse Spirit of Lee come my way, and together with good old Jungle Bunny I have horses to take abroad on which I can make a suitable showing.

So, looking back, what seemed at first to be a complete disaster may in the end prove to be a blessing in disguise. I have learned a great deal – especially about making sure that I have horses under contract, so that I can continue to ride them once I have brought them to the peak of performance that is required for modern-day show jumping.

Pam has managed for the first time in our married life to have a family life. She only goes jumping when it pleases her, rather than doing it as a necessity or under pressure. She can now give much more of her time to Robert and the change in him has been dramatic. When you are at the top of the sport you do miss a very great deal. There is no real home life and, despite having a very good nanny in Kate Davis, there is nothing for a growing little boy like having his parents about for at least half the week rather than one day a week as it was before.

How do you finish a book about your life? I want to finish mine on a note of success and hope for the future. Amazingly, that turned up one day in the late summer of 1984 just six short months since we lost all the horses save Jungle Bunny. The phone rang and I answered it, a bit reluctantly like I always do because the phone is constantly ringing in our house. However this time it was worth answering for it was Jackie Wood, the International Affairs Secretary of the British Show Jumping Association, telling me I had been picked to join the British team to go to Lisbon at the end of September.

This was great because although I had been to several invitation meetings abroad during the year and had done pretty well, it is a different thing altogether when the BSJA recognize that you have once again become a force who can represent Britain abroad. This was a full CSIO and without doubt the Spanish would field their strongest possible team seeing that Portugal is on their doorstep.

After the initial feeling of excitement and hope, however, I found that the cards were still stacked against me. I had two horses that I thought were Grand Prix standard – Jungle Bunny and Synapse, but a week before we were due to leave for Portugal I was having trouble in keeping Synapse sound. So I rang the Association asking for permission to take Spirit of Lee instead and they gave the go-ahead. Then the day before we were due to leave it appeared in the press that Jungle Bunny was going abroad with me. Within a short time Tony Elliott was on the phone to say I couldn't take the horse abroad because he was too old! Unfortunately, because Jungle Bunny, whom I had ridden for all these years, had been jumped under the name of Griffin and Brand, that, in the eyes of the BSJA, makes them the owners. I was desperate. I rang Elliott and pleaded with him to let me take the horse. The answer was no – full stop.

One of the many reasons which Tony Elliott gave for this bombshell was that he didn't think Jungle Bunny would stand the long journey to Spain. Yet in May his other horses – my ex horses remember – were sent on a long tour of Spain and seemed none the worse for the experience.

It also transpired that he thought the CSIO in Lisbon was a very minor event despite the fact that we brought back the Nations Cup to Britain after a lengthy absence. He suggested to me that I was only picked for this because no one else wanted to go – something the following paragraphs will easily refute. However there was another even more sinister reason for his objection. If I jumped Jungle Bunny in Lisbon I might conceivably get a double clear and so qualify the horse for the Horse of the Year Show and he told me quite bluntly that he did not want to see me jumping at this top notch show.

Now it subsequently got back to me that the reason why Griffin and Brand took all the horses was that Tony Elliott wanted the publicity that would go with having several of his mounts jumping in the Olympics. For various reasons, which we needn't go into, eventually none of his horses jumped in the Olympics. That was a supreme disappointment to Tony and such news travels fast through the grape-vine of the show jumping world. Through keeping my ear to the ground I discovered that I was taking the brunt of his disappointment at the dashing of his Olympic hopes.

However you cannot keep a good Dunning down and I still had the untried Spirit of Lee. I contacted Ronnie Masserella. 'If you think the horse is Grand Prix standard,' said the British *chef d'équipe*, 'then that's good enough for me.' He confirmed it with Lt.-Col. Blacker and we were on our way to Lisbon with all our eggs in one basket.

Even when we got to Lisbon there was still a doubt as to whether I would jump in the Nations Cup even because, unless circumstances prevent it, there are always more riders than are required for the team.

So the Grand Prix on the Saturday was crucial for my chances. I had to do well. However, by that time I was feeling pretty confident. When you have only one horse then you make doubly sure that you are getting the best tune you can out of that animal. On the Wednesday opener Janet Hunter, the Scottish Ladies' champion, jumped into third place with the Spanish and Portuguese dominating the field. I was tenth but better things were to come.

On the Thursday Michael Mac on Packers Hill won the competition and I halved my previous score and came fifth, while on the Friday I made eighth, but it is he who laughs last that laughs longest. I was feeling really confident in Spirit of Lee. The thirteen-year-old was jumping wonderfully and, I had to admit, better than Tarzan would probably have done in the circumstances on the fairly firm going.

The course for the Grand Prix on the Saturday was

enormous. It was bigger than anything Spirit had jumped in his life, but that did not deter me. I knew that I had to do well because so many things were likely to depend on this showing. If I was to remain an international then here was the testing ground and the horse seemed to know it too because he pulled out all the stops and we ended up with just one rail down in the first round and a good clear in the second. You have to understand that this was Spirit of Lee's first major international competition abroad. He had never done anything quite like it before and he acquitted himself magnificently.

I just beat Janet, who was really on form, by a couple of seconds and we two ended up third and fourth respectively. The event was won by Belgium's Michael Blaton on Waigon who had two clear rounds, but the second one was a bit slow and he ended up on three-quarters of a time fault. Alberto Honrubia from the Spanish team was second. Michael Mac got seventh place so the Brits did very well and we began to look like a real force to be reckoned with. As well as those mentioned we also had Gary Gillespie and Graham Fletcher, but the results of the Grand Prix had picked the British team and I was one of them. Now I had to use all my experience and low Dunning cunning to make sure that Spirit did as well or even better tomorrow in the big one.

You can get horses that jump clear given the time, or horses that can cover the distance but not jump the height. On the Grand Prix course we had to do both as the Portuguese course-builder, Colonel Luis Moura Dos Santos, made sure there was no time to spare at all. At the same time he made sure that the fences were as massive as before. It was going to be a very tough assignment. To make it more difficult the comparatively primitive arrangements meant that there was no display clock by which you could judge the time that had elapsed. Anyway Michael Mac jumped clear in the first round on Packers Hill, Gary Gillespie had a rail down and Janet Hunter on Lisnamarrow was a second outside the time and got a quarter of a time fault. Spirit jumped out of his skin to make that another clear for our team, although you wouldn't have thought so because when I came out of the ring feeling pleased with myself I got the biggest wigging from Ronnie

Masserella I think I've ever had. It appeared that I had cut it
so fine that I was inside the time by just one hundredth of a
second. I must say that hurt a bit but I came back at him.
'Well,' I said shrugging, 'what are you worried about – I was
*inside* the time wasn't I?'

So after the first round the British stood in a really strong
position as we could drop Gary's four and end up with just a
quarter fault. However, the Spaniards were living up to their
name as favourites because they ended up the first round on
zero having been able to discard Rutherford Latham's cricket
score of twenty-three on Jacaranda.

The second round was crucial and once again Michael
jumped clear, Gary had two down and half a time fault and
Janet gained another magnificent clear.

I came in late in the round and knew what I had to do. If I
jumped a clear we would win the Cup and if I had just one rail
down we would end up second because the Spaniards had
collected a total of three-and-a-half penalty points in the second
round. The pressure on you under normal circumstances is
massive when you get into the anchor-man situation. For me,
with my international reputation to regain, it might have
become unbearable. Maybe more unbearable for those watching than for me though, because when you have been in this
situation all your life you learn to throw off the pressure and
concentrate on the job in hand.

Actually no one dared tell me when I went in that things
were as tight as they were and so maybe that helped to turn in
the second of my clear rounds that day to clinch the competition.

I expect it has become clear to you by now that the accolade
in Nations Cups is awarded for jumping double clear rounds.
There are very few of them and you remember the ones you
jumped very clearly, but I doubt if I shall remember any double
clear (even the three double clears in one season that Jungle
Bunny gave me) with any more affection than this one.

OK. I'm in my mid forties, the way back up is tough, but the
Doc says I needn't retire until I'm sixty – or more! So who
knows where the boy from the small town in Hampshire will be
by then. The young tearaway who threw up home, family, even

jumping, to find himself – and then nearly lost himself – has had a life of massive ups and downs, but even now I feel as I take stock this far along the way that I really have been 'Dead Lucky'.